Irma Was Here

A Personal Story

Surviving the Eye of History's Strongest Atlantic Hurricane

DIANDRA JONES

ISBN 9781794569454

DEDICATION

I dedicate this book to the people of Puerto Rico who welcomed us with open arms—only eight days before meeting their own devastation at the hands of Maria.

ACKNOWLEDGMENTS

I would like to thank my husband, Adam Stauffer, for barreling through the waves of life alongside me with quiet wisdom and always, a tight embrace. Too soon in our married life did we face challenges that are statistically unbeknownst to most couples. As I surmised, we stayed the course, and are still navigating with our joined hands on the helm.

To our families as they watched us, with worry, wander far from home, with horror as we disappeared below a bloody red blob on a radar screen, and with enduring love as they continue to help us rebuild our lives. In the days immediately following Irma's impact on our home, the island of Tortola, our stateside family entered a disaster zone of their own— fraught with communication breaches, misinformation, terror and helplessness. It is only because of their support have I been able to write this book, or do anything of consequence in my life, come to think of it.

Thank you to my kindred spirit Kate Lotz, who anchored me in tumultuous weather through my early thirties, when we were both drifting souls on the island of St. Thomas. The kind of friend that life bestows on the lucky, Kate not only sheltered Adam and me when we had no home, but seems to have a heart that can harbor the world.

To Tanya Merchant, my fellow English teacher in Raleigh, North Carolina, where Adam and I took refuge after Irma. Tanya turned from stranger to friend when she delicately delved into my personal story, liberal with her literary expertise and lovingly light with the red ink.
Thank you, dear Ms. Merchant.

Finally, to our beloved community of Cane Garden Bay, Tortola. If I managed to capture even a sliver of your beauty, your charm, your vitality, then it was worth my while to write this book. One of my greatest fears as I witness this dangerous brewing concoction of climate change, apathy and oblivion, is the possible loss of idyllic places like Cane Garden Bay—where exists true ecological and social symbiosis, where a simpler, more altruistic way of life has been preserved, where the beauty of the natural environment is reflected in the smiles and wagging tails and flapping wings of its residents.

PREFACE

June 1st, 2018

Dear Reader,

This is not a great survival story. But it *is* by far the most difficult thing I have ever written. I am not pulling debris from wounds or learning to walk again. But I am healing in another way, as are, I am certain, all my fellow Irma survivors. And it is a healing process that may not be noticeable to the eye, but please know, it is still happening, and will continue to for years, maybe decades…

Having to recap this horrific historic incident has been gut-wrenching. Many times, I wanted to walk away and allow myself to move on. To relive the tragedy of Irma each time I sat at my computer, no matter how pristine or functional my surroundings were, was oftentimes unbearable.

Why did I ever take the time to write this? Hours of time and physical and emotional energy that could have been spent moving forward, looking for a new home, a new job, new friends, new dreams, new scenery—were stolen from me because of this book. Irma took more than my home away from me. She took away my sanity. And then this book took away my time to heal.

I have to remember why. Why did I first sit down to start recording these events? Now I remember—first it was out of a sense of helplessness. In the immediate days, then weeks, then months after Irma decapitated Tortola, most of our friends were still there. Many never left. Weren't we lucky? To get the hell out of there, and leave behind the place and people we love while they were down. Weren't we even luckier? To have been among the teeny-tiny percentage of the human race to experience the eye of history's strongest open Atlantic hurricane. (Note to the future: Stop killing the planet or we may all join that narrow percentile of "lucky ones.")

We felt completely helpless, and shell-shocked, and guilty. I wanted to scream to the world, HELP THEM!! WHY ARE YOU JUST STANDING THERE? PLEASE HELP THEM. On Facebook community boards I savagely bit tourists who pondered when the sailing season would pick back up, or wondered has anybody seen my boat? Screw your boat. My friends are thirsty. My friends don't have a roof and another hurricane is coming straight for them. (That was Maria). I held fundraisers. I poured my own money and time and energy into raising awareness and funds for relief efforts. I obsessed. I made videos. I didn't sleep much. I drank a lot.

So that was my motivation at first. To solicit help. Then it was to recount and make sense of it all. Post-traumatic stress has made that very difficult. I cannot believe how many terrible details my brain has tried to erase in order to let me heal. Between Adam and me, we have had a difficult time piecing together the sludgy pulpy pieces of Irma's sick puzzle. Tortola will spend the next decade piecing herself back together, and that puzzle will never look like the picture on the box. It may not even come close.

And then my motivation was to heal, but only time will tell if this process has been consoling or cathartic. I would argue the latter.

The last three months this book has sucked my soul from me, to the point where I've dreaded opening up this file, having to backtrack and proofread and edit. To reposition commas and delete spaces from a pussing, oozing wound. Then is when I truly needed a reason to keep writing. And finally, it was this:

As months faded and so did Irma, I have been amazed and saddened how quickly Irma has eroded from the media and public consciousness. An American man we met while exploring Nicaragua as a possible new home, weeks before the country fell into political upheaval, said to me, "Dude! You went through Irma?! That must have been AMAZING!" I nearly vomited. Months prior, a kind-hearted Yoga teacher, benevolently leading a fundraiser class for Irma survivors, guided students into Palm Tree Pose with the

mantra: "Palm trees sway and bend, but they never break."
My inner Zen was all that restrained me from commenting,
"Actually, palm trees *do* break." Guess who could break them
all?

Irma. Who was so powerful she registered as an
earthquake on the Richter scale.[1] Irma. Who has scientists
proposing new building codes be enforced in hurricane-
prone communities and a category-6 and 7 be added to the
Saffir-Simpson scale. Their hesitation lies in the fact that the
Saffir-Simpson scale is designed to measure the potential
damage of hurricanes to human-made structures. Since
sustained winds over 155 mph (category-5) will rupture
"hurricane-proof" structures in as little as six seconds, a
higher category is deemed useless. Even the home of
acclaimed country singer Kenney Chesney on the island of
St. John, designed to withstand 200 mph winds, was
breached by Irma's ferocity, his expensive high-tech windows
sucked out in seconds.[2]

Categories of hurricane

	Category 1	Category 2	Category 3	Category 4	Category 5
Wind	74-95mph	96-110mph	111-130mph	131-155mph	Over 155mph
Storm surge	4-5ft	6-8ft	9-12ft	13-16ft	Over 18ft
	Minimal: No real structural damage; some flooding	Moderate: Material damage to buildings; small craft break moorings	Extensive: Structural damage to small houses; inland flooding	Extreme: Major structural damage & heavy flooding; evacuation necessary	Catastrophic: Massive damage to buildings; small structures blown over or away

Source: Saffir Simpson scale

Saffir-Simpson Scale. PA Media. @pa. "The latest storm
sweeping over the Caribbean." 19 September 2017. Twitter.
https://twitter.com/pa/status/910083721394565121

---

[1] Estes, Steve. @seismo_steve. "Seismometer recordings from the past 48
hours on Guadeloupe show Cat. 5 #Hurricane #Irma driving closer toward
the Lesser Antilles. " 5 September 2017. Twitter. https://twitter.com/
seismo_steve/status/905049088642703362

[2] "Country singer Kenny Chesney's Virgin Islands' home destroyed by Irma."
CNN News Source. 12 September 2017. www.ktnv.com/news/national/
singer-kenny-chesneys-virgin-islands-home-destroyed-by-irma

When it comes to raw strength, Irma has few rivals, throughout history. Only 33 Atlantic hurricanes have ever earned category-5 status. Of those, only 18 broke wind speeds of 175 mph or greater and only seven topped 180 mph or greater. Of the 15 eastern Pacific hurricanes considered to have reached category-5 status, only five broke wind speeds at 175 mph or greater. And most storms that would qualify for the title of category-6 were typhoons in the western Pacific, most infamously the titan, Typhoon Tip, of 1979, which sustained winds of 190 mph, and typhoons Haiyan and Meranti in 2013 and 2016, respectively, with sustained winds of 195 mph.[3]

Hurricane Irma was a record-breaking mutant and a harbinger of what is to come. Born off the West African coast on August 27th, she was nursed to monstrous proportions by unusually high sea temperatures and light winds in the upper atmosphere, and on September 5th, 2017, matured into the strongest hurricane ever recorded in the Atlantic basin, outside of the Gulf of Mexico and the Caribbean.[4] She then proceeded to break another world record when she became the strongest hurricane ever to make landfall in the Caribbean [she is the second strongest *landfalling* Atlantic hurricane—1935 Labor Day Hurricane in the Florida Keys, the first], slamming the Leeward Islands [Barbuda, Saint Barthélemy, Saint Martin, Anguilla and the Virgin Islands], and then barreling through just north of the islands of Puerto Rico and Hispaniola.[5] Finally, Irma broke her last record to become the longest-lasting category-5

---

[3] "Saffir–Simpson scale." Retrieved 12:02pm, July 28, 2019. Wikipedia. https://en.wikipedia.org/wiki/Saffir–Simpson_scale

[4] "Hurricanes and Tropical Storms - Annual 2017." National Centers for Environmental Information. National Oceanic and Atmospheric Association. https://www.ncdc.noaa.gov/sotc/tropical-cyclones/201713/

[5] Henson, Bob. "Category 5 Irma Hits Leeward Islands at Peak Strength." Weather Underground. 6 September 2017. https://www.wunderground.com/cat6/category-5-irma-hits-leeward-islands-peak-strength

hurricane in recorded history, when she maintained her rare 185+ mph category-5 winds for 60 hours.[6]

In my pre-Irma days, I may have apologized for boring you with scientific data. But Irma has sucked away my aptitude for unnecessary apologies. Like *Gone With the Wind*, all I can say is, "frankly, my dear, I don't give a damn." I have grown tired of holding my tongue or downplaying Irma's record-breaking magnitude. I have grown tired of rushing through my response to the question, "Where did you move from?" because I realized people were bored before I even finished the sentence.

"My husband and I lived in the British Virgin Islands but Hurricane Irma destroyed the place." How fast can you say that? I have learned to say it pretty fast.

But in this book, I'm saying it slow. I'm stretching it out syllable by syllable, as if speaking to a child.

Please, world, put down your toys and listen. Something historic and horrible has happened. An unprecedented barrage of the strongest and deadliest Atlantic hurricanes in recorded history.

Hurricane Harvey

Hurricane Irma

Hurricane Maria

Take heed. Because it didn't come out of nowhere. It came out of climate change. What else but the freakishly warm sea temperatures could have fed this beast, giving Irma the strength to mutate from a storm of 100 mph winds to a monster of 185+ mph winds, in less than 24 hours? (Another science lesson: warm waters intensify the updrafts that lower barometric pressure inside storms, creating stronger winds.) An average hurricane can expend energy the equivalent of 10,000 nuclear bombs in its lifespan—Irma had heated to an unprecedented catastrophe of nuclear propensity, literally overnight. Planet Earth is cooking, and

---

[6] Chappell, Bill. "Hurricane Irma Blasts Into The Record Books With Lasting Intensity." NPR. 12 September 2017. https://www.npr.org/sections/thetwo-way/2017/09/12/550188154/hurricane-irma-blasts-into-the-record-books-with-lasting-intensity

our love for cars, coal plants and red meat made this microwave. It was us who injected Irma and her siblings with the steroids of global warming, and then it was us who took a beating.

And we had better hope and pray it doesn't happen again. But if it does, here's a guide, to prepare you for the many ways that a catastrophic hurricane could rearrange your life.

I repeat. This is not a great survival story. Adam and I were lucky compared to most. Read "Irma's Diaries" by Angela Burnett Penn to hear true Irma survival stories. (Yes, our story is included, and you will see, it pales in comparison to others). This book is one person's account of what Hurricane Irma did to her home and to her heart.

CONTENTS

PART I: IRMA

CHAPTER 1: WE JAMMIN STILL

the building
could fall down
we jammin still
we jammin

the treasury
could burn down
we jammin still
we jammin

-Lyrics of *Full Extreme* by the Trinidadian Band Ultimate
Rejects, Dubbed the Anthem of 2017 Carnival

The day is Sunday, September 3rd, 2017. I drive my patchwork black 1992 Suzuki jeep, nicknamed Zorro, carefree up and down the lush green hills of Tortola, British Virgin Islands, into its sunny pastel center, Road Town. There are two passengers in my backseat: an elderly lady on her way to church, and a teenage boy going to "lime with his friends in town," both neighbors to whom I've given lifts before. Even if I hadn't recognized them, I would have picked them up. Tortola is safe. Tortola is my home. I love this island and the people. In fact, I love Tortola even more when I have company with whom to share its beauty on my way into town.

The sunlight that soaks our atmosphere, the Soca that sweetens our airwaves, the tepid turquoise sea unveiled at each crest, the cozy sweep of coconut trees cocooning our journey, and the azure sky that envelops our world: all testify that life is good. I am sure I am smiling.

Daily radio broadcasts advise the public to stock supplies: one week's worth of food and water, a flashlight with extra batteries, duct tape, weather radio, matches, first aid kit, toilet paper, sunscreen, rope, etc. The Department of Disaster Management warns us that this hurricane season has a 45% chance of being above normal, due to elevated sea surface temperatures. Such is the background noise of a Caribbean summer.

My passengers alight with gratitude at the bottom of Joe's Hill and I carry out my Sunday errands in town. My mind churns choreography, in preparation for this week's upcoming adult dance classes.

A close friend messages me with urgency to ask, "Where will you be staying?" She tells me her family has relocated to what they deem is a safer place.

"At home," I respond.

I decide it best to pick up another gallon of water and some more canned food at Bobby's market in our picturesque home of Cane Garden Bay. As is common in Tortola, I greet several more familiar faces—it is actually more uncommon to see faces you do not recognize—also stocking up. I find the shelves emptier than usual, and I'm grateful to find a few remaining gallons of water in the back of the store.

From the quaint sea-level coastal road in Cane Garden Bay, lined with homes and villas and beachside bars, I wind my way up our steep, crumbling road behind the usually vacant police station, back home where my husband Adam works quietly at his computer in our simple, one-bedroom villa. The exterior French doors facing the ocean are open wide, inviting sea air and sun to bathe our front room with light and love from our island paradise. Just beyond, our balcony gapes over a life-size canvas of green, gold and blue brush strokes; a span of tropical vegetation descends into soft sparkling white sand: tiered seating for the most stunning show on earth, the Caribbean seascape.

My dance students now message a steady current of compassion and concern to one another.

"Does everybody have someplace safe to go?"

"Be careful everybody!"

"Make sure you are all prepared… good luck everyone."

This class of adult men and women called Tortola Dance Project has grown close over the past several years, although not exclusively through our weekly classes and monthly performances. It was nearly one month ago, August 7th, 2017, that together we danced through what was the worst flood in Tortola's documented history. An unprecedented and unforeseen 17 inches of rainfall in under 17 hours drenched the island and the hundreds of parade participants who marched unsuspectingly through Road Town's main thoroughfare in the annual Emancipation Festival.

Initially only slightly deterred by soaked Carnival costumes, runny mascara, and droopy feather headpieces bleeding blue dye, we sensed true danger when water levels rose suddenly from ankle-level to waist-deep, ghuts overflowed, submerged cars floated from their parking spots and drifted away. Dancers piled into cars to race back to their homes, if they were able to go home at all, as many structures at sea-level were under water or mud. Tortola, a usually pristine island with scarce litter or unsightliness, was now caked in muck. Electricity was lost in many areas of the island, roads impassable, trees down, and a reported $50 million worth of damage to personal property and businesses. It was unimaginable for an island to flood so severely. Small islands have plenty of places for rainwater to go. They are surrounded by ocean. For hundreds of years, Tortola's mountainous terrain and natural system of ghuts had efficiently channeled rainwater safely back to the sea.

This time, it was just too much water in too short amount of time. The island could not handle it.

In the following weeks, food and clothing donations from the U.S. Virgin Islands and Puerto Rico poured in, and gradually debris from the roads was cleared, as drivers were advised not to venture out in order to allow the Department of Public Works to do their job. The below-ground level of Elmore Stoutt High School, Tortola's only public secondary school for roughly 1500 students, had filled nearly to the ceiling with flood water. Several of us dancers along with other volunteers helped in its cleanup, which seemed impossible. Nearly a one-foot layer of suspicious septic sludge lingered, a smelly murky mess through which we sifted, laden with classroom items and whatever else, alive or dead, that happened to have been swept by flood water down the hills and through the ghuts to finally mummify in mud in these catacombs of erudition.

Heartbroken teachers beseeched us to salvage what we could from the excavation site, and scoop the rest (mud and all) into garbage bags, which were then hauled in continual trips by a single wheelbarrow to an onsite dumpster. Committed to and exhausted by this seemingly endless task, I spent five hours sweeping, hauling, power-washing, scrubbing and sifting, often gagging at the odor and nebulous lumps of questionable refuse my fingers blindly fumbled from the sludge.

Both the Premiere and the Minister of Education and Culture, on their rounds across the island to inspect damage, stopped by to grin and pose, holding shovels, for the local paper. By the time I had left, I walked away weighted with defeat, feeling too small to help in such a colossal undertaking, feeling that the island, perhaps, was too small…

Jamaican dancehall music beckons us like Odysseus's sirens from Myetts beach bar below, intermixed with the occasional laughter of Sunday afternoon revelry. We know our dear Guyanese friend, Vishaal, is serving cold beers and our friends and neighbors will be carousing until nightfall. Adam and I attempt to exercise discipline and stay at home for the remainder of the evening, opting out of our normal

Sunday romp at the beach. He immerses himself in his work. I lackadaisically sweep the floor and tidy our tiny home, grateful for a boring end to a beautiful day, a welcomed break from our sometimes overwhelming social lives.

One dancer sends out a recent news article from the Orlando Sentinel, stating that Irma, the ninth hurricane of the season, has been downgraded to a category-2 Hurricane. However, she is predicted to gain considerable strength on her traipse towards the Leeward Islands. (That's us.) Bafflingly, the Global Forecast System of the [US] National Oceanic Atmospheric Association (NOAA) and Europe's models show Irma heading in different directions. It is unclear if Irma will veer our way or not. Hurricane Harvey, having just drowned Houston, Texas, not to mention media coverage and public attention, also drained the U.S. government and American people's sympathy and humanitarian coffers, and has now, much to the country's relief, fizzled into a tropical depression glazing over Louisiana and Mississippi.

I glance over the article as I hum along to my own 2017 Soca playlist booming from my laptop and bouncing me into dance. This particular song wins my attention.

the building
could fall down
we jammin still
we jammin

I set down my phone, and "wine my waist" around our front room, singing loudly, reviving choreography from that fateful Carnival. I still marvel at the fortitude of the dancers that day, and the island's own considerable fortitude after such a blow from nature. Adam's gaze remains fixed on his laptop, my impromptu solo dance-parties a regular fixture of our home. In fact, our wifi password is "Dance Party."

Outside, bananaquits and doves lilt a blasé tune. From our balcony, I scan the horizon to see the magnificent frigate birds hovering effortlessly on updrafts, and pelicans nosediving for their dinner like kamikazes. It appears that all is well.

"Let's go down for one," Adam suggests. "Who knows? It may be awhile before we can go out again."

Maybe the Soca music swayed him…

I am easily persuaded, throw on one of the few dresses I own, flip flops, and lipstick. Adam and are I minimalists. It takes us seconds to get ready and head out the door. We have few possessions, one of the commonalities that initially attracted us to one another. I had grown used to simple life from my time in Ghana, where I inhabited a small room in a compound with a communal outdoor bath and toilet (hole in the ground), shared by four other families. Adam had downsized his entire life to a 37 foot sailboat during his one-year sail around the Caribbean. The first night Adam and I spent together, I swooned at how nonchalantly he shared my toothbrush, and that he did not own a wallet, his credit cards and cash swaddled by a rubber band. We share a tiny single closet, all of our meals, and still to this day, a toothbrush.

Adam and I find our friends before the sun sets, Vishaal greets us with a bright smile, and Sunday night unfolds in its typical joyful fashion. There is moonlight, dancing, singing, socializing, warm sand and cold beer, on one of the most beautiful beaches in the world. Perhaps we all enjoy each others' company more than usual tonight. Everyone seems to recognize how good life is, and how lucky we all are to be here, together, on this little rock.

The following day, Monday, September 4th, Adam withdraws a precautionary $400 from the ATM. After hours of visits to Immigration, the Labour Department and the Social Security Office, he obtains the forms he needs to request his annual work permit renewal. It is a grueling song and dance of its own kind that all non-residents, known as "non-belongers," begrudgingly trudge through each year in order to inhabit an island they love. At the largest grocery store in Tortola, Riteway, he stocks up on water, canned goods, matches, candles and a flashlight, then fills the car's fuel tank, and finally returns home, doing his best as man of the house to prepare his domain.

"Heard you guys are hanging in there? What!?" My dear

Aunt Betsy in Baltimore sends her well intentioned horror via email. She tenderly suggests we take haven with family in the States.

We've been through hurricanes before. The British Virgin Islands have always evaded harm. This will be no different. I don't have time to write her back. I have my life to attend to, choreography to craft, music to arrange, important things to do.

I do take a quick glance at an online storm tracker— Irma has now been upgraded back to a category-3. Earl in 2010 had been a category-4, and we survived with minimal damage. I remain calm.

By midday, the Governor of the British Virgin Islands, the hand-selected representative of Queen Elizabeth II, officially announces that all government offices will close this afternoon at 4:30pm to allow public officers to finalize their own preparations for Irma. Furthermore, all residents of Anegada, the northernmost and flattest of the British Virgin Islands, are advised to leave the island and take shelter with family and friends.

The soporific shushing of ocean waves and swaying palm leaves that waft up from the shore below sound no alarm. Nor do the sunbathing lime-green noles that stalk our ledges and walls, awaiting their next feast from the unsuspecting mosquito.

As Adam and I prepare dinner, we take a break to step out onto the balcony and watch that glorious sphere of gold dip its toes into the sea, then gradually disappear, casting its last rays of serenity over our horizon. Tree frogs break into their nightly serenade and temporarily chirp away my fears.

My phone incurs a barrage of messages into the night, from increasingly concerned friends and family.

"Are you prepared?"

"Are you staying?"

"Get out of there."

My mom sends one final message of the day: "I will pay for your flights, to anywhere you want to go." I tell her I'd like to leave, but Adam wants to "ride it out."

I decide to call my boss, the founder of the British

Virgin Islands Dance School, Sandy Lyons, to ask her if I should cancel tomorrow's adult dance classes, to allow people more time to adequately prepare for the storm. She sighs her response: "Well, it probably wouldn't be a bad idea."

When I alert my students, a few respond with disappointment, but understanding. I wonder if I have made a mistake, and decide I will certainly feel foolish if this storm turns out to be nothing. Adam and I nestle snugly into our bed and, because we've never owned a television, watch a movie on Adam's computer until we fall asleep.

CHAPTER 2: TURNS OUT TO BE SOMETHING

On Tuesday, September 5th, 2017, I awake furled and framed by Adam's warm fuzzy body. It is hot. In the tropical heat of endless Indian Summers, a single thin layer of linen atop lovers can feel smothering. Our windscreens languidly sip in a breeze the flavor of soursop trees and sunshine. Even in the heat, I would normally lay still, rocked and soothed by the gentle ebb and flow of Adam's chest against my back, waiting for my love to wake, so together we can start our today.

But today is different.

I reach for my phone moments into consciousness and check the online storm tracker.

"Wake up," I tell Adam, as I stand and begin shoveling clothes into a duffel bag. "Irma is now a category-5. We're heading to the airport."

As Adam packs, I frantically book two online tickets to Raleigh, North Carolina, where we can stay with my younger brother, David. He is already housing my cousin, Margot, who evacuated Miami yesterday. In my frenzy, I mistakenly book the ticket for the wrong date—but we don't realize this until later, when it is, perhaps, too late.

I have visions of wind—powerful wind—that sweeps over the island, turning everything into confetti. Irma is coming.

It is funny—I never hated Irma, the way so many people did before and after the storm. I feared and was in awe of her. I felt like I was about to face God. And me, what am I? Sure, within the communities where I have lived, I may have been of some value. But now it was time to feel my part in this universe. Small. Like the leaf blown from the branch into the ocean, to drift away and disintegrate into nonexistence. Like the mosquito that buzzed my ear in my sleep, driven by thirst, indifferent to its odds, squashed in an instant between my hands, and in less time, forgotten.

Irma, compelled by no vendetta, was about to squash us with her two hands. Of this I was certain. As to what could we do about it, I was uncertain.

But I did not blame her. It was not personal, it was nature. Human beings are vicious compared to Irma—we harm, destroy, sabotage and murder for personal reasons, not even for survival's sake. Irma would sweep through and level our self-important, self-destructive constructs of civilization, with no judgment, no wrath, only sheer ambivalence. And with all of our great inventions, our clever ways, our obsession with ourselves and our own self-worth, we could do nothing about it.

I message my family to tell them we are coming. Adam rises from bed—thank God—I think, relieved that my sometimes too easy-going partner finally feels some sense of urgency. We finish packing our bags, cramming in only a few articles of clothing, important documents, old family photographs, and our precious electronics—iPhones, laptops, hard drives—modern virtual keepsake boxes. Vestiges of our own life's meaning and legacy.

It is with great shame that I drive us through and out of Cane Garden Bay. With every neighbor I pass and wave to, as is my habit in Tortola—it is a 21 square mile island with a population of roughly 25,000 people; every inhabitant is in fact, your "neighbor"—my smile cloaks writhing feelings of cowardice, betrayal, selfishness, and fear, growing fear. As though we are stealing the first lifeboat off the Titanic.

At the Terrence B. Lettsome airport on the East End

of the island, we arrive a half-hour later. On our way we pass a jam-packed parking lot at the Riteway, sweating men on ladders boarding up windows, and the typical throng of pedestrians, some in business attire bustling to work, others strolling leisurely, lounging on porch steps, sipping from cracked coconuts on the corner.

The airport is surprisingly quiet. Flying directly out of Tortola is expensive—usually a last-minute resort for the budget traveler. A ferry-ride to St. Thomas, U.S. Virgin Islands, although inconvenient, offers a more affordable exodus to the mainland. Somehow, I am not in a thrifty mood today and have fronted nearly $400 each for two one-way tickets to Raleigh.

I approach the United counter where a tall slim young man looks at me with puzzlement. The time is 10am.

"Good morning. Please, I just booked two tickets to Raleigh on the 11:55am flight." He peers over his shoulder to whom I presume is his superior, an expressionless plump middle-aged woman who is too preoccupied to notice his distress. Offered no relief, he returns his glance to us.

"I'm sorry, but the last flight of the day is boarding now, and it is full." Adam and I see a short line of passengers edging through security.

"I don't understand—I just booked these tickets." I step aside to view the flight schedule for the day, and can see plainly that there are no more United flights scheduled.

"Are there any other flights out of here?" Back at the United desk, I plead to the apologetically helpless young man. His superior now stands beside him and confirms the truth to which I must yield.

"The airport is closing at noon today so *we* can prepare for the storm," she relays to me with less sympathy, more finality, and an acute ambiguity.

Who does she mean by *we*? The airport? The airlines? Or is she referring to herself and her coworker? Her grave face begs me to picture their families, their homes, their own personal need to close shop and get the hell out of here. I withdraw my case and back away from the counter.

A smaller airline, Air Sunshine, is the only other counter

where there are still agents behind the desk, and a growing line of anxious customers queueing up.

"Let's go," Adam says, and we join the row. As we wait, I check my phone for the flight I had booked earlier in the morning and see that I had, in fact, booked it for September 21st, the wrong date. I admit it out loud, with confessed stupidity and repentance. Next I message my family members and ask that they look for flights for us—out of Tortola or through St. Thomas, it doesn't matter. Even to Dominica. This may be our last chance. Just get us out. In the survival mode of fight or flight, we are about to lose the latter option.

One relieved customer at a time, the line in front of us peels away. Air Sunshine lights up their faces, promising escape and safety. Even as my family abroad fails to find us other evacuation options, Adam and I grow hopeful as we near the glowing beacon of Air Sunshine.

I recognize a teenage student from the local international school standing immediately in front of us, with her mother and father. We make eye contact and I am about to say "Hello! Hope we all get out of here," when she turns away to face forward. Finally, they reach the counter, receive their tickets to Puerto Rico, and step to the side. We are next.

The pretty agent with soft thick curls that fall to her shoulders looks sadly at us as we approach. "I'm sorry, there is only one ticket left." Adam immediately tells me to take it, but I cannot even entertain the thought, envisioning the unbearable torture of being separated from him, as he weathers Irma alone. Not an option.

"That's okay, thank you," I respond to the agent, with hopes that there is a single traveler somewhere behind us in line who can take that ticket. I glance behind us and see only couples in line. As we walk away, I hear the sun-kissed, gray-haired pair behind us in straw hats and linen shirts tread that difficult conversation, as the Mister says to his Missus, *please take that flight.*

CHAPTER 3: FIGHT OR ~~FLIGHT~~ COWER

In the months after Irma, only a few times have I questioned our decisions leading up to, and following, her indelible visit. Second-guessing now seems as futile and dangerous as it would have been to try to predict which way Irma would fling the cutlery from our counter as she threw her tantrum in our kitchen. Best to safely hide the cutlery in the cabinets, and secure them well. Very well.

But in the 24 hours before her arrival, there was a lot of second guessing. Should we try to catch a private boat? Should we try to find a place to stay that is more solid? Should we have tried to find a life plan that was more solid?

Only a few weeks prior, Adam and I had taken our second look at a home we had hoped to buy. It was within walking distance to the water, which was important to us, as we considered what type of life we wanted for our future children. (Ironically, we never once assessed the house's "hurricane-proofness"—such was the rarity of destructive hurricanes in Tortola.)

Married three months prior in June 2017 at ages 41 and 37, respectively, Adam and I were now beginning to try our best at "settling down," a process that did not come naturally for either of us. Adam had been a Wall Street trader whose disillusionment during the economic crash of 2008 drove him to buy a 37-foot sailboat with a childhood friend, learn how to sail, and then proceed to sail the entire Caribbean.

In 2008, I had left my teaching post in Chicago to move to Ghana, West Africa, where I taught HIV/AIDS awareness, studied dance and taught at the international school, operated a motorcycle touring company for three years, and then moved to the U.S. Virgin Islands. Adam and I met accidentally in Tortola during the Fall of 2013. He had been contemplating a return to his native San Francisco. I had pit stopped in the British Virgin Islands to choreograph for a local dance company, on my way to a new teaching post on the tropical African island of Mauritius. He asked me my name, and I asked him to dance. It was soon clear that our wandering paths would be consolidating, perhaps for life, and that Tortola would be our home.

Proximity to a surf beach was key to Adam, who grew up surfing in California and Hawaii, and was ready to reclaim that passion, providing a much-needed diversion from the stress of running his own asset management company. Community was key for me. Three years of village life in Ghana had impressed upon me a value and lesson that I hoped to never relinquish—the virtue of communal life, which still existed in many parts of Tortola, especially in Cane Garden Bay, where we currently resided.

Another priority for us was the ability to house family. Age and travel, as it tends to do, imbued in us a keener kinship with mortality and distance—and suddenly, after a decade of spotty Skype calls from faraway hostels, internet cafes, coffee shops and tiny, temporary apartments, we wanted to close the proverbial and geographic gap between our progeny and predecessors. If we were going to have a family and live on a tropical island 2000 miles away from Gramma and Grandpa, we had better have a home where Gramma and Grandpa could make themselves cozy, for long periods of time.

While we had only been waiting for some final documents from the realtor before we were ready to make an offer, there was an unmistakable and unexplainable hesitation within me—not only because I was snug in our Cane Garden Bay abode—it was something else, something that to this day I cannot call by name.

It seems to be getting hotter and I am frazzled. And quite frankly, I am tired of having to make all the decisions. Why did I listen to my husband and wait until the last minute to evacuate? Why did I have to make the decision to leave? Why did I have to book the flights and hurry us to the airport? Why has the fear of death and the responsibility of survival been placed solely on my shoulders? When you are handed such heavy tasks, you are also handed the blame if your decisions prove faulty. My fried brain desperately cries to be "tagged out" of this match against Irma, in which I am quite obviously the weaker contender, and seem to be the only player on my team.

Less than a mile from the airport, I pull over the car and succumb to tears. "YOU DRIVE," I snap with anger and resignation.

Adam does not own, nor has he ever owned, a driver's license. But he's not a bad driver. He just chooses to walk where he needs to go, as one less vehicle clogging the road and polluting the air. From the passenger seat, I slowly begin to calm myself down from the adrenaline rush of escape mode, and reset my flurried heart and mind to our next plan, whatever that is, unaware that my quiet husband is harboring a secret. Adam has been mentally preparing for this day, following the fluorescent fetal blob of Irma on the weather radar as she crawled and kicked and mutated into the full-grown beast that she is. While the whole world seems to be dumbfounded by her freakish development, my husband had never taken his eyes off Irma's incubation. He has imagined what was unimaginable and is mentally ready. I am not.

My loving mother sends message after message of suggestions. She and my devoted team of three brothers are looking for ferries, private boats, even private planes off of this island. Unbeknownst to us, they are embroiled in a frantic debate over what Adam and I should do. They are ravenously researching, pressed by the looming possibility of our imminent deaths.

My younger brother, David, envisions our house slipping away, plowed by a mudslide, the two of us inside, crushed. He is voting for us to move underground, a basement if possible. Or he recommends we park our car near our window between us and the mountainside, to act as an external barrier from a crumbling Earth. My older brother, Darren, tries to recall from his fleeting visits the exact location of our house on the hillside, the angle it faces, the degree to which it juts out from the hillside, how exposed we will be to the herculean winds barreling our way. He votes for us to relocate to someplace lower, shielded within a valley by other structures, by the mountainsides themselves. They all agree that we should seek a stronger, more protected, more fortified place to stay. It's difficult to determine if and where a place like that—impenetrable to the leviathan indiscriminate force of Mother Nature—exists.

My mom scours outdated websites for a list of hurricane shelters on Tortola. One of them is a large church in Cane Garden Bay on "the flats" (flat coastal land), less than 10 meters from the ocean. This sounds like a horrible idea to us—particularly if the storm surge is significant. Truly, unless it is a solid underground concrete bunker, it will be no better than any place else. But still, I ask Adam to drive to a hotel/restaurant on the East End not far from the airport to inspect it as a possible refuge. The owners, who know us well, are grimly packing up tables and chairs and tell us all the rooms are full. They use the day's standard greeting, "Sorry, be safe," and Adam and I begin our drive back home. As time to prepare our own home is slipping away, rather than drive all over island to find what we may haphazardly deem a safer spot, Adam calmly convinces me to instead fortify our homestead as best we can.

With our proverbial tails between our legs, we drive back through Tortola. I am embarrassed and wonder if anyone we meet along the way can sense that we just tried to flee in terror. As we pass Tortola's locally owned version of Home Depot, called CTL, we see trucks loading up with lumber, and further along our route, even more men sweating on ladders boarding up first, second, even third story windows. People finally seem to be barricading and burrowing into some semblance of safety.

In Cane Garden Bay, again, we stop at the local shop

and buy even more water, some batteries, and cigarettes and beer. We also grab more canned food: baked beans, ramen noodles, eggs, bread, Campbell soups, and charcoal for our small grill. One usually lighthearted, comical friend from the UK checks out in front of us. She jests with sarcasm, "Be safe," then pauses and adds with less jest, "God, I'm so sick of hearing that. To be honest, I'm scared shitless." Amongst her checkout items are two cartons of cigarettes. We head back to our bunker.

Along the road, we pass our landlady, who assures us that our windows are hurricane proof and we don't need to be worried. Upon arrival, our only neighbors who have not evacuated our building also assure us of the structural soundness of our home—concrete walls, concrete ceiling, hurricane proof windows, steel rods running throughout all the way down into the earth to anchor down our home from blowing away.

"These homes are not made flimsy like they are in the States. These homes are built island-strong, for withstanding hurricanes," our dreadlocked Tortolan neighbor tells us. We find comfort in his words.

Taking instruction from online hurricane-preparedness guides, and the endless torrent of advice that streams in from my family—much of it contradictory—we mentally and rapidly sift through an overload of information on how to prepare for a category-5 Hurricane. We also monitor weather updates from various trusted online hurricane trackers and weather reports to gauge exactly what we may be up against.

A 12:45 p.m. report from the National Oceanic and Atmospheric Administration shows the eye of Irma, now the strongest hurricane ever recorded in the Atlantic—outside the Caribbean Sea and Gulf of Mexico—due to pass straight over the British Virgin Islands, with sustained winds of 185 mph, and gusts reaching higher.

My family tells us to tie ropes around our balcony to help deflect debris, board up doors and windows, shield them from the inside with mattresses, furniture, clear building materials from the construction site immediately downhill from us, perhaps use pieces of it to help barricade our home.

First, we bring in everything from our front balcony that could possibly become projectiles—a table and two chairs, a giant ceramic vase, Adam's surfboard. This is standard procedure, even for a category-2 Hurricane. We decide to leave Seymour, a perched wooden parrot suspended from the ceiling of our balcony, as an experiment to see where he ends up—it's a futile attempt at humor to calm our jumbled nerves.

We criss-cross our windows from the interior with strips of duct tape, and scan our front room for other objects that could become dangerous flying debris. Really, at 185+ mph, anything hurling towards you will hurt, maim or kill you. So we clear our kitchen counter and dining table, and stuff all loose items into the kitchen cabinets along the floor—in case our hanging cabinets, themselves, become projectiles. Whatever is too large to store there we shove into our armoire, including my guitar, all of our books, ranging from Yoga manuals and Caribbean Dance Anthologies to Business and Economics books, and a few pictures—one recently given to us by my mother—a framed photo of us, the only one we own actually, as bride and groom on our wedding day.

I have an African drum that, like Irma, has traversed the Atlantic. An ornately hand-carved, 20 pound, two-foot tall djembe, it has traveled with me for the past ten years— having been lugged from Ghana to the U.S.A. to the U.S. Virgin Islands, back to Ghana, back to the U.S.A., and then finally, like me, found a home with Adam in this Tortola apartment. While I have left behind many of my prized possessions for the sake of life adventure—a piano, a well-worn bicycle, a Chicago park-side apartment, several motorbikes, my lovers, my friends, my family, even my career —I have never left behind this drum. Except for one time.

Adam had to shout over the booming dancehall music at Le Grande Cafe. He was stunningly handsome. I was hiccuping. I think he said he wanted my number? If only I could remember what it was.

"I DON'T KNOW IT. I'M ONLY BORROWING THIS PHONE!!" is the only information I could succinctly communicate through the late night haze of loud lights, loud music, loud conversation, loud personalities—all amplifying proportionately to alcohol intake. So he tried another approach, stepped aside and asked my friend Meagan, who coincidentally had told me six months prior that she knew a guy who would be good for me. As it turns out, Adam was the guy.

"BE A MAN!" Meagan bellowed at him. "ASK HER YOURSELF." Adam tried again.

"WHAT IS YOUR NUMBER?!"

"I TOLD YOU! I DON'T KNOW IT—hiccup hiccup." He is adorable. I am hiccuping. I need to go home now before I humiliate myself. And so Meagan and I left the bar. Although Adam at this point believed that he had been rejected, he thankfully did not give up.

Over the next couple days, Adam tried to reach me, and he got my number finally from Meagan. Within a few more days we were living together, my red canvas suitcase hidden in the shadows of his bedroom. I was careful only to pull articles from it as I needed, keep it zipped, my belongings hidden away, not strewn about his room. Like my possessions in that red canvas suitcase, I would surely be in and out of this place. And I would soon be out of sight. But for now, isn't it lovely to get to know this man?

Days passed—we woke up together, we fell asleep together, we worked side by side together typing away on our laptops. I was writing what I predicted to be the next great American memoir of my motorbike adventures in Africa. Surely, my life had been so exciting. Surely, it would be a best-seller. And then on to my next great adventure.

Adam was watching the stocks, watching world events, predicting whose fortunes would crash and whose would catapult them into caviar. Our own fortunes were unfolding, and weren't we fortunate.

However, my temporary work permit with the local dance company was soon to expire—the performance was over, my job done. Christmas was approaching and I would follow the plan: holidays in Pennsylvania with the family, then perhaps teaching in Mauritius, or earn a PhD, or…

But I left my drum. For the first time since it became mine, I left my drum. With Adam. To anyone who knew me well, this was a sign that I would be back, not only for that drum, but for that man.

I think of this now as I drag it into the corner of our apartment, its very presence a reminder of Adam and my past, and my own transition from a wanderer to a wife. The ancient Adinkra symbol that embellishes its Twenoboan wooden body is called Mmusuyidee, a crusader's cross-like figure that signifies, "That which removes bad luck." It is a Ghanaian cultural emblem of good fortune and a sentimental memento of Fortune's benevolent intervention in my own life. It's hard to imagine it becoming a deadly weapon, flying through the air to bludgeon us. I nestle it into the corner of our bedroom, hoping that it doesn't end up killing us.

It is a strange process to sift through your possessions, rearrange your furniture, and think, "Will this kill me? How about this?"

We push our heaviest furniture up against the windows, as a last possible barrier between us and external debris, in case our doors and windows shatter or break. I snap some photos of our pre-Irma redecorating efforts to share with my family and assuage their anxiety—our armoire barricading our french doors, no longer open and inviting to a gorgeous seascape, now a blackened eye in our usually bright, sunlit home.

Our pull-out bed/couch we push against our side set of french doors, and our dresser up against our bedroom window, with a Yoga mat wrapped with duct tape around the mirror. We yank the mattress from the pull-out couch and shove it in between the bedroom window and the dresser. We stack all of the pillows from our entire home neatly on our kitchen counter immediately outside our bathroom door. If every barrier is breached, our last resort is to hide in the floor of our shower, where we will use these pillows to cover and protect ourselves, along with our mattress. This, of course, will hopefully not be necessary.

There is a relentless inner battle of wits when one is gradually and methodically preparing for an oncoming, unavoidable natural disaster of monumental proportions. One side of your brain laughs, taunts, condescends to the other: "You are overreacting. Don't be ridiculous. You will be fine, you big baby."

And in actuality, there is still a chance that this hurricane, like most of its predecessors, will veer away from the British Virgin Islands at the last minute, and we will only be peripherally hit. Although, my brother Darren has already told us the size of the storm is also unprecedented (it is now the size of Texas, its eye 25-30 miles wide), and regardless of where it turns within the next 24 hours, we will still be hit.

The other side of the brain, however, has already fast-forwarded to sheer terror, is screaming, running, shredded by debris, bloodied, bashed, gouged. The shit has already hit the fan. This side is saying: "You fucking idiot. You didn't prepare well. Now you are going to die."

Adam cleans the toilet, duct tapes our shower curtain to cover the bathroom window in the shower stall, and removes the sliding doors from our shower, to make more room for our pillows and mattress, if it comes to that. He also opens our kitchen drawers immediately outside our bathroom door so that they are slightly ajar, blocking the bathroom door from flinging open. I keep thinking of the men we passed boarding up windows, and I want him to do the same for our home. He insists that it's not necessary. "It wouldn't hurt," I plead. "It's not necessary," he repeats himself for the last time, as the tone of his voice suggests.

I think to myself, I should do it myself. Am I helpless? Do I need a man to do this for me? But we have no lumber. I'd have to drive all the way back to town, and even then we have no hammer, no nails. We need a drill. The walls are concrete. Will the nails even go in? Maybe I should just trust my husband.

Adam takes the car to refill the fuel tank in case there are fuel shortages or outages in the days to come. Also, our car may be our only source of news, via the radio, and power to charge my mobile phone and help us stay connected. When he returns, he clears the rest of possible flying debris that our upstairs neighbors had left in the yard, one of which is a 3-gallon bucket full of bolts, nails and springs. Then we begin stashing food and water in various parts of our apartment, in case one part is destroyed, and the other salvaged. We place a gallon of water, some snacks, a plastic ziplock bag containing our money, passports, credit cards, car keys, phone, phone charger, a sewing kit, hydrogen peroxide, as well as the remaining duct tape, rope, exercise resistance bands, a hammer and candles in our bathroom cabinet, in the extreme case that this is the last standing portion of our home, or worse yet, if we become trapped in there. The sun will be setting soon. We have prepared as well as we can and decide to head down to the village to share libations, perhaps one last time, with the neighbors of our Cane Garden Bay community.

Just before we leave, a mutual friend of ours writes from afar: "I would be most worried about the chaos after the storm hits. The crime, the desperation, the mistrust. Things are getting bad in St. Maarten. The people have turned on each other. Be safe."

CHAPTER 4: ONE LAST STROLL

Two nights after our first encounter at Le Grande Cafe, Adam and I rendezvoused on the beach in Cane Garden Bay. It was past midnight and the sea was exceptionally angry. She was roaring and rising and slamming herself down against the shore, shaking the earth and pounding our eardrums. Such was a rare sight in Cane Garden Bay, whose tranquil clear turquoise waters typically tip-toed on and off the shore.

We sat side by side in silence, looking up at the stars, clearly in love with each other, and in love with this place.

"Let's go for a swim," Adam surprised me.

"Okay," I eagerly complied.

The waves were the biggest, in fact, I had ever seen them in my three years living in the U.S. Virgin Islands. And yet we plunged through the dark torrid waters, further than I usually would swim, particularly at night, and particularly in waves that high. Laughing, we ended up in an embrace, our legs and arms wrapped around each other, bobbing and buoyed by the warm saltwater, when we were pummeled by the first giant wave. Somehow we maintained a loose, easy hold on each other, our bodies relaxed as they submerged and rolled beneath the waves. In slow motion, together, we gently bounced against the soft sandy ocean floor, and resurfaced moments later, still hugging, still laughing. And so it went on like this, wave after wave, we surrendered to each other, to the powerful sea.

Stepping onto the beach now, I glance towards that spot where we have since sat so many times, gazing out to the ocean, and up to the stars. It is not "our spot." It is here for everyone. Every sunburnt tourist sipping the island's signature cocktail Painkiller, every tropical-shirt clad bartender asked to painstakingly serve them, every father teaching his boy to swim, every girl cartwheeling across the sand. Every expat lawyer and accountant who weekly trade their business suits and briefcases for bathing suits and beers. Every construction worker, carpenter, plumber, politician, electrician, artist, doctor, dentist, veterinarian, chef, chiropractor, school-teacher, principal, car salesman, mechanic, musician, seamstress, custodian, landscape artist, architect, hair stylist, fisherman, massage therapist, police officer, engineer, boat captain, sailor, secretary, photographer, physiotherapist, nurse, every nanny.

Here is where we all come together each Saturday or Sunday afternoon to "lime" together and enjoy the beauty of this little island paradise. Tortola is actually the first place I have resided where every person from every walk of life can sit and chat and be seen as equals. A friend of mine from Jamaica, who has traveled extensively, once commented that Tortola, compared to other Caribbean islands, was unique in this regard. It is one of the many reasons I love this place.

As the sun starts its arced descent back towards the sea we are not alone to soak in one last sunset on this special beach before it may cease to exist, at least, the way we know it. Among its admirers tonight are the principal of the international school, an American, and his Italian wife, whom we catch in a romantic embrace at the shoreline. Without trying to intrude, we greet them. He remarks, "Came to take one last look," to which we solemnly nod with unspoken understanding.

Also canoodling at the scene, his belly stretched along the cool sand beneath a lounge chair, spooned by his best friend Victor, is Tanner, a tawny beach mutt and one of the regulars at this beach. Not dissimilar in appearance to most of the stray dogs on Tortola, Tanner and Victor both resemble Corgi mixes, with pointy ears, a slender short-haired small body and stumpy legs. (Victor, the more social and mischievous of the two, is a Corgi-pitbull mix). It is rumored that these Corgi concoctions are relics of English colonization when Corgis, the prized pet of the Queen, were popular pals of English explorers and settlers. Tanner waves his tail when he hears our voices and wiggles from his cozy beach-bed, outstretches his body in a Yoga downward dog and yawns an audible squeaky sigh of sheer contentment.

Tanner has a good life. Like many of the beloved beach dogs at Cane Garden Bay, he roams freely every day along the beach, fed pizza and chicken wings by sunbathing tourists; stroked, hugged and coddled by countless adoring local and vacationing children, and fed proper dog food morning and nightly by at least one local family. When he is hot he saunters ten feet to the lapping waves and cools himself in water that was designed by Mother Nature to be the perfect temperature for an overheating body. When he is hungry, he snuggles up to a human, either foreign or familiar, and waits for his irresistible cuteness and good manners to take effect. When he feels like playing, he joins the other free (and claimed) dogs as they race along the water's edge, wrestle in the sand, nibble on each others' ears, charge, sniff, and naturally, hump.

Tanner has no master. He is a free dog. He belongs to no one, and receives love from everyone. He is unclaimed not for absence of willing foster parents. Adam and I have taken him into our home on several occasions, given him a collar and name tag, provided for him a comfortable bed, freshwater and food, only to find him patiently waiting at our front door each morning, longing to rejoin his friends and his freedom at the beach. He loves his life and his neighbors (both human and canine), and simply because he gives and receives affection, does not suggest he needs or wants an owner. Cane Garden Bay provides him with all the ideal ingredients of a dream life for a dog: sustenance, beauty, companionship and love.

Tanner may look similar to the other beach dogs, but he is special to us. And, like typical egocentric humans, we believe we are special to him. When he hears our car rumble along the road from 100 meters away, he stops, turns and waits for us, waving excitedly (with his tail, of course) until we approach. Tanner embodies qualities that are rare to find in any living being: an indomitably positive spirit, loyalty, goodwill, infectious happiness, enduring love, and an unconquerable will to live.

One day upon returning from a week-long trip to the States, we found Tanner hiding alone under a tree alongside our hillside road. Worried when he didn't come to meet us, we crawled under the brush to discover Tanner had been hit by a car, his back hip badly injured, his tail, still wagging. Even then, he only allowed us to carry him home and nurture him for a day, before he limped back down to the beach the following day to heal himself in his place of happiness.

Mere weeks later, I found myself in a difficult situation. My car was at the garage, a common destination for old island cars, which take a regular beating from rough island roads, and there were no passing cars from which to hitch a ride. I had to trudge up the long hot winding road on foot, which is grueling on any day. But on this day, I was lugging behind me a 50 pound suitcase. Tanner greeted me at the foot of the hill and proceeded to limp along beside me in the heat, dragging his back leg for the entire 30-minute trek up the steep, shadeless undulating road. When I feared I hadn't the stamina to make the summit, I looked beside me at Tanner's broken body, his bright brown eyes shining at me, his waving tail signing to me, "We can do it. Keep going! We are nearly there!" I thought to myself, if this tiny disabled dog, my little guardian angel, can climb this hill—out of free will, not even necessity—then I certainly can do it too. Why did he accompany me? He would not accept water or food once home, but immediately turned back down the hill to the beach. Why? Not out of obedience. Not for reward. To this day, I can determine only one possible explanation. For love.

A couple years later, I was driving at night along the road, and Tanner, per usual, waited for my car and then began running alongside of it. I slowed down, shouted at him through the window, begging him to stop, as it was dark, and we were nearing a curve where oncoming cars were blind to cross-traffic.

"Tanner, stop! Stay Tanner! Stay!"

Just as we approached the curve, Tanner darted across the road, and to my horror, an oncoming car swung around the corner, slammed on the brakes, but not before its back wheel churned over Tanner's back leg. I shrieked and stopped the car. Tanner yelped and scurried into the dark bushes. The passing car also stopped, the driver stepped outside, stricken with guilt and shock and probably stunned by my hysteria. I called Adam and after thirty minutes of searching futilely for Tanner in the dark brush, I had to meet dancers in town for a performance. Adam returned later that evening, found Tanner, and carried his injured body, still alive, back to our home. Again, after only a day or two, Tanner recovered and sat at our door, eager for his good life to carry on.

As Tanner trots beside us now, tail wagging, Adam looks to the sky and observes that the frigate birds seem to be flying erratically, not elegantly hovering and swooping as usual. If we hadn't the modern technology to inform us that something unnatural was about to occur, these haywire frigates would certainly have been a sign.

Tanner also breaks pattern and prematurely parts company halfway down the beach, we assume to find a suitable place to wait out the storm. We pitstop at the roadside bar "Paradise Club" to congregate with Tortolan families who have resided in Cane Garden Bay for several generations. Despite our relative newness, obvious transplants to this intimate community of extended families with hundred-year lineages easily identified by surname, we have never felt alienated here. We have never been treated as tourists, or even transients. Greeted with smiles, and the standard "Good morning" or "Good evening" Caribbean greeting, we have been made to feel a part of this community.

Leaning on the wooden U-shaped bar under a palm-leaf roof, they joke and drink and discuss what last preparations they still need to make to their homes. The elderly man who sits beside me is complaining loudly and with jest for all the women to hear.

"I have to sleep by myself tonight! Oh, poor me, poor me. I have to go home and sleep alone."

The women simply laugh, as he orders another drink. He next declares that he will be finishing this drink and heading home to climb his ladder and fix a window. This alarms all of us, as it is almost dark, he is almost drunk, and Irma is almost here. He insists he will be able to do it, but then repeats his primary concern, "But poor me! I have to sleep alone!!" and winks at one woman between pretend sobs.

Our landlady joins us, and soon after, several more friends wander up to the bar. Our plump and jovial friend Kay, a boat captain from Cornwall, asks Adam and me if we had seen the video footage of Barbuda, an island 196 miles southeast of us, being hit by Irma a few hours ago. When we reply, "No," she responds: "Oh good. If you haven't seen it, then don't. Spare yourself—can I get a shot?"

The bartender pours her a shot, which she swings back like a reflex, then lights a cigarette. Grabbing her beer she exclaims, "Cheers to everyone! Tomorrow, we're all fucked." We all raise our beers and toast.

"But please, show us the video," I press.

Kay refuses again and again, but finally acquiesces. "Okay, I'll show you, but believe me, you don't want to see this."

Holding her phone in my hands, I watch in horror at an island, just like our own, being torn apart in seconds. Literally, seconds. One moment there are leaves on the trees, the next moment, there are *NO TREES*. It is like nothing I can even imagine. It doesn't even seem possible. I am speechless. I pass the phone to Adam to watch, and step away from the bar in shock.

"And that was only a category-4," Kay bellows from the bar. With my beer in hand, I light my own cigarette. Adam joins me, and lights one as well. "Holy shit," he says, and we smoke in silence.

My mind turns to all my friends who have children.

Here we are boozing at the local bar—what are they doing? Reading bedtime stories? Watching cartoons? I fear gravely for Adam's life and of course, my own, but I cannot begin to fathom what it would be like to have children. How can they possibly protect their children from that type of brutal power? To extend this grim feeling of helplessness to something as precious and vulnerable as your own children, who through no choice of their own are spending their childhoods on this island—a place they were born or brought to by their adventurous, free-spirited, roving parents, who sincerely believed they were offering their children a better, more idealistic upbringing than their own.

Adam and I had always admired the family life of Tortola-dwellers, and aspired to provide the same atmosphere for our own children someday. Kids on Tortola were remarkably respectful, worldly but grounded, connected to nature, appreciative of the life they lived and well aware that not all kids get to grow up in such an idyllic place. They grow up surfing and swimming in the ocean. Their birthday parties are gigantic Caribbean sea "pool parties"—the kind I would have only dreamed of as a kid growing up in dreary Erie, Pennsylvania. Island life is perfect, until it is not. Only on the rarest occasions can paradise transition so quickly into a living hell. I know I am not alone with this sick feeling grinding my stomach and my mind into mush. It is palpable here amongst everybody. We laugh and joke and swig beers to mask our fear and the very real reckoning that this may be our last hoorah.

I take a seat back at the bar, hoping the rollicking old man will lift my spirit and calm my nerves. He has already ordered another beer, and now he is talking again about that window he must fix. "I been meaning to fix it for years—I don't know why I waited." He takes a sip of beer. The ladies are now paying their bill and saying their goodbyes. He turns to me and says quietly, "I normally don't get afraid of these hurricanes. The BVI has had so many." I nod with understanding, feeling ill-equipped to remark. He adds, "But now I am afraid. Now I am afraid."

He pays his bill and leaves his beer half-full at the bar.

One of the women walks him to his car and soon I hear them laughing again. An unfamiliar young man stands on the periphery of the action. I approach him, and ask him if he's visiting. I can only assume so since I've never seen him before. A muscular, sandy-haired, 20-something year-old white man, he seems awkwardly aware of his otherness, chuckles nervously and scratches the back of his neck, although I am certain it does not itch. Soon when I hear his story, I realize why he is in such a state of discomfort, even more than the rest of us.

"Actually, it's kind of a funny story," he begins, chuckling nervously again. He clears his throat, as panic itself seems to block his windpipe. "So I was delivering this sailboat from France, and was supposed to drop it off in the British Virgin Islands," he pauses, swallows, and continues.

". . . but then Irma came along, and we've been trying to outrun her for the past week across the Atlantic…" he pauses again, and looks around as a few more people have crept up to hear his story.

"I'm Diandra, by the way," I take a moment to try to make him feel comfortable—as much as I can upon first meeting—like he is among old friends.

"Oh hi," he laughs again, "I'm Murray…Yeah, so we had to outrun Irma," he continues, "but there was no wind. It was crazy," he begins to speak with more vigor, as though he is reliving the past six days, as though he is back on that boat, out on the open sea in the middle of the Atlantic Ocean, being chased by the strongest Atlantic hurricane in recorded history.

"We were hoping to be able to get to another island, out of her way, but Irma was gaining on us, and we didn't want to meet her at sea, so we rushed to shore here," he gulps, "in her direct path, to try to secure the boat and take shelter." Moments of silence pass as we all stare, speechless, at poor Murray. He fills the silence, "We just arrived this afternoon." His small audience of unabashed eavesdroppers mumble disbelief and condolences to the visibly shaken visitor.

"You have someplace to stay?" someone asks.

"Murray's staying with me! I got him!" Kay sweeps beside him and wraps an arm around his back.

"He's in good company!" She squeezes him closer to him and hands him a beer. We all raise our beers to cheers to Murray, and he smiles genuinely this time. The unmistakable altruism of his onlookers finally disarms the stranger.

Soon after, Adam and I decide to say goodbye. We zigzag Zorro back up our hill through the dark, park the car several feet away from our neighbor's, our windshield a giant lens for the moon-streaked sea, then park ourselves on our balcony to absorb the night's majesty.

Following my mother's advice, I charge our computers and phones inside. I occasionally step into our apartment to message my family, and leave Adam out on the balcony alone. I am torn between wanting to stay in touch with them for as long as possible (we are certain the winds will begin shortly, and the electricity will be cut once the winds exceed 65 mph) and wanting to savor these last moments with my husband in this home, before Irma may make new life plans for us, that is, if our lives are still ours to plan.

I write my family, "I am trying to be optimistic, but I seriously don't know if we're going to make it. I love you all." And then I pretend to joke, although Adam and I have sober-mindedly discussed this, that Adam was pre-med in college and can stitch us up with our sewing kit if need be.

I message my childhood friend who lives in Florida and ask her to please evacuate. Somehow, I will feel better enduring this beast if I know Irma is not on her way to kill my friends and family stateside. If there's anybody whom I can protect—unfortunately, there's nothing I can do for my friends here on Tortola—I try to do that now. She asks me how I'm feeling. I respond, "I'm scared. I'm scared that the people I love on this island will be hurt, or die."

Our nephew from Pennsylvania writes, "I just wanted to send you a message before the storm hits to let you know that I love you so much and I'll be thinking of you guys. Stay safe, you got this!"

My younger brother David writes, "Diandra. I would tell neighbors and friends that you are riding it out in that back bathroom. In case debris/trees/mud come down at all —I don't think it will. But better to be extra cautious."

I thank them all for the steady influx of love and testify that it is bringing comfort. I think about anyone who has to weather through something like this alone, like the old man from the bar, and my heart sobs.

"It is scary, and it is natural to be scared" my mother concurs. "I think when this is over you and Adam should leave and visit David in North Carolina as there is another storm, Jose, behind it but not as strong." There is no room in my mind to contemplate the ensuing hurricanes, nor the armageddon that may accompany a complete and total destruction of our island.

My family continues to lend advice, which I relay to Adam who rests in silence, gazing out over the ocean from our balcony. I can tell he is growing increasingly annoyed by the endless suggestions, whereas the constant communication brings relief to me, as well as my family. At least a slow-moving oncoming disaster allows loved ones time to comfort each other, offer advice, maybe even say their goodbyes.

I take comfort particularly in one new update they tell me, that Richard Branson has decided to stay in his island paradise home on his island of Moskito, in the BVI. Certainly, he had the option to leave, and yet he has chosen to stay. Now, like every other resident, he is stuck on an island, facing a historically mammoth storm, and like us, he is probably afraid.

My brothers have been communicating with my 71-year-old dad, whom I tried to reach earlier in the day, and they ask him to call me. His voice instantly brings tears to my eyes, but I try my best to subdue my emotions and not worry my loved ones more than necessary. This will be a continuous effort in the days to come, an ongoing attempt to filter our worst fears in any communication with our family, and temper our desperation. If we are going to die, there is no use in dragging your family through the slowly unravelling horror that precedes such a bitter end.

My dad tells me he's going to come down from Erie,

Pennsylvania in his fishing boat and rescue us. I laugh heartily, a standard response to most of what my dad says. Then he asks how we have prepared, and I tell him our step-by-step preparations to set his mind at ease.

"And if worse comes to worse," I add hesitantly, wondering if this detail is necessary, not only in our preparations, but in relaying to my poor dad who can do nothing to protect his daughter from far away, "we will hide in our tub surrounded by pillows and our mattress."

With his familiar fatherly way of setting his "child's" mind at ease, he assures me that we have done all we can do, and we will be okay. He next begins to tell me a story from his days as a helicopter door-gunner in Vietnam. When I was a kid, my dad would often tell me Vietnam stories—none too gruesome, but still probably painful stories he kept in the caverns of his heart and mind that, over the years, his memory had deemed worth storing, and his judgment, worth resurrecting in order to share with his little (and only) girl.

"One night we were all in our bunker and we were getting hit. Rounds were going off all around us, and everybody grabbed their guns and took their places to fire back. Except for one guy. He was terrified, so he ran and jumped into a corner. We didn't want him to die so we covered him with mattresses and pillows. The shooting went on for at least an hour, and finally the enemy retreated. And guess what..." he pauses, adding suspense as a natural storyteller...

"Only one guy was hit. Guess which guy that was!?!" He starts laughing and pauses to cough a little, indicating that maybe it's been awhile since my dad laughed this hard. I imagine my dad's face, his own blue sparkly eyes filling with tears, and his gap-toothed smile stretched wide across his bright youthful face—at least that is the impression he is giving me. Of course, I know that my dad is also trying his best to filter his fears, and just keep me calm, and laughing.

"That guy hiding underneath all of those pillows! He took a bullet in the butt, went home with a purple heart... Can you believe it?" I laugh some more. "Aaaah man, isn't that something?!" my dad concludes his tale, still laughing and sighing, "Aaaaah man…"

So, I gather, the lesson here is: if debris comes flying towards us, best to take the brunt of it in the rear-end. I laugh with relief until the joke's temporary distraction expires.

I must interject that I do not mean to trivialize any injury, or death for that matter, that was caused by Hurricane Irma. Many people were injured terribly and some were killed by flying debris, and perhaps worse than dying, people watched their loved ones die. There would be nothing funny about flying debris in the unleashing of Irma on the British Virgin Islands.

I have nothing more to say to my dad, but don't want to end the conversation just yet, his voice and his presence, even if from 2000 miles away, an unequivocally soothing antidote to my growing unease. My dad has endured endless traumas in his life, his service as a helicopter door-gunner in Vietnam undoubtedly the foremost and perhaps largely responsible for the slew of self-induced adrenaline-driven accidents that followed. He understands life or death situations, having experienced countless of his own. And he understands and respects nature and its insurmountable force. He spent much of his life on the open water of Great Lake Erie. At the very least, he understands wind. I did not need to convey my fears to him of what 185 mph winds could and would do to this island, possibly to our home, to us.

I remember as a child, my dad took us four children out to Presque Isle State Park, much against my mom's wishes, to experience the force of remarkably strong and rare winds sweeping over Lake Erie, the fourth largest great lake, and 11th largest lake in the world. We had to hold hands and form a human chain as we leaned into the wind and climbed out of our family station wagon onto the beach. There are eleven beaches along the peninsula that juts out into the lake, and my father drove us only to the first beach, perhaps because he knew the severity. Sand whipped our faces and my feet felt as though they may lift up off the ground at any moment, the force unlike anything I had (yet to) experience.

Suddenly, a deep unnatural groaning sound pierced the air, and my father commanded loudly for us all to run back to the wagon. At that moment, an 8-ft tall sheet metal fence along a beachside condo began peeling away like tinfoil from leftovers, and hurled up into the air, nearly hitting my father, as we turned to race back.

My dad, of course, acted as though that sort of thing was normal, although we were all stunned silent, and I am quite confident that none of us ever relayed that part of our family field trip to our mom, who sat at home anxiously awaiting our return.

He now tells me how lucky we are to face Irma in the daylight. "Imagine going through something like that at night!"

It's a valid point and brings a morsel of comfort. Once more he assures me we will be okay. I cannot tell if he is faking conviction, but I am not convinced. I think back upon my unconventional life choices, heavily influenced by my fearless father whose own body is a roadmap for the unconventional, reckless lifestyle—each broken bone, every scar a landmark for some past exploit, some of which we know the backstory, some of which we will never know.

Finally I utter, "I'm sorry," and choke back tears.

"Ah," he says softly, "For what?"

"For putting myself in this situation, for the stress it may cause my family…"

He cuts me off, "You didn't do anything wrong. And you and Adam will be just fine. You've done all you can do and you will be just fine."

Our conversation ends shortly after, and my brothers echo my dad's sentiment through more messages.

"You and Adam are smart and resourceful."

"You'll be okay."

"You'll get through this."

As a Yoga and Dance teacher, I know the power of words and positive-thinking, and the mind's ability to subdue the body. I can self-soothe all I want, but I am not foolish enough to believe that I (or any human) has any control over Mother Nature. Whether Irma finds us meditating serenely in a bathtub, or shrieking in terror, she will find us. We are simply in her way.

I say goodnight to my family. Then Adam and I relish one last view from our balcony and say goodnight to our Caribbean nightscape. Waves gently crawl on and off the shore. Palm leaves sway and whisper. The moon watches over, casting a kind and cool silver light to usher us back into our home, where we now commence lockdown.

It is a strange feeling to close every door, every window, and cut off the fresh night air from penetrating our home. To separate ourselves from our natural environment was far from the reason we chose to move to such a place, where the body and its surroundings are in constant equilibrium. Adam and I have never had to wear a coat to warm us. We have never used an air conditioner to cool us. In fact, in the ten years I have lived in the tropics, I have never used an air conditioner. A refugee from bitter cold snowy winters of Northwestern Pennsylvania, I cherish an open-air home, to feel the breeze, the heat, even the humidity, to smell the rain and the fruit trees, to occasionally find outdoor critters (lizards, scorpions, sometimes birds—once we even had a wild goat end up on our balcony) inside. So this should be a small sacrifice. To have enjoyed 365 days of harmony with nature each year, for the past ten years, certainly I can endure a few hours of discord.

We turn on our small standing fan near our bedside to offer some circulation. With all the windows sealed tight, it does not take long before our bedroom becomes a sweatbox, but Adam and I somehow manage to sleep, aware that at any moment the world outside may turn hostile.

CHAPTER 5: BIG BAD IRMA

"Little pig, little pig, let me come in!"
"Not by the hair of my chinny chin chin!"
"Then I'll huff and I'll puff,
and I'll blow your house down."

Three Little Pigs, Fable from *Nursery Rhymes of England*,
Published 1886

We wake to sunlight and silence. Maybe Irma has missed us. Maybe she has dissipated. Maybe all the weather reports were wrong. Then I notice the fan has stopped, which means the power must have been cut, which means the winds, over the course of the night, must have surpassed 65 mph. I turn to face Adam, who still sleeps. I wrap my arms around him, press my chest against his and kiss his neck. Then I slip out of bed and open our bedroom door. Now I hear the wind. My phone tells me it is 9:42 a.m. I open our side door cautiously and a strong breeze rushes against me. However, it seems safe to step out onto the balcony and so I take the chance. Trees lean in accordance to the wind and fling a few of their leaves up into the swirling air. This is the beginning.

I decide to quickly make breakfast for Adam and me. I silently debate whether to fill our bellies in case it's a while until our next meal, or save our food if it's a while until we can get more. On our gas stove, I fry two eggs and two pieces of bacon. I try not to open our fridge more than necessary to prevent the cool air from escaping. In case of a prolonged power outage, we hope to delay the rotting of our perishable food supply. I recall a BVI-born friend recounting how category-4 Hurricane Hugo in 1989 knocked out Tortola's power for an entire week. Adam has placed two gallons of water in the freezer to turn to ice and help preserve the cold.

Although I had lived in Ghana without consistent electricity for several years, foregoing refrigeration all together, there lies greater peril in being power-less, while being simultaneously isolated. Not only is the island isolated from the outside world, but individual families and residents may also become cut off from other parts of the island, as mudslides and fallen trees could block people from entering or exiting homes.

I hear Adam rustling, and soon he enters the kitchen in his boxers.

"Has it started?"

"Yes," I respond, handing him the breakfast. "Take a look for yourself."

He sets the plate down, and I follow him to our balcony where we venture to witness the arrival of Irma, for as long as we can.

The sun gradually disappears as menacing gray clouds encroach the sky, and our world darkens. Dwarf cyclones chassé across the bay. Howling winds lift and launch ocean water hundreds of meters, spraying the entire mountain side. Trees spasm and spew their leaves into more violent gusts of wind. Adam runs inside to grab our GoPro knock-off video camera. I dress myself in jeans, thick socks and high-top sneakers, atypically heavy attire for a Caribbean environment. In case we need to make a run for it, I want to be ready to bound over fallen trees, broken bits of home, my flesh and soles of my feet protected from debris on the ground and in the air.

We take turns scarfing down our breakfast, sharing one plate as we always do, while the other watches on the balcony to monitor Irma's offensive. The wind shrieks, and a vortex of levitated ocean water and rain whips around us. The particles streaking through the air, once clearly identifiable as leaves, are growing larger, darker and less identifiable. Pieces of who knows what careen past us. I recall from the video of Barbuda how rapid was the progress of Irma's destruction, from airborne leaves, to branches, to entire trees ripped from their roots and syphoned into the atmosphere.

Adam stands beside me now, filming, ravenously soaking in the phenomena. His excitement temporarily offsets my urge to run and hide. With trepidation I linger, straddling exhilaration and fear, hypnotized by Irma's conjurings, yet poised to bolt at any moment. Finally, something the size of a small dog whizzes past our balcony, and I decide it's time to retreat. *If Irma could pick that thing up and throw it into oblivion, it won't be long until she can do the same to us.*

"I'm going to stay a little longer," Adam shouts, entranced by Irma's miasmal, cosmic display.

I fear that my husband believes he is enjoying the show of a lifetime. In flashes, I see him as a child, his face pressed up against glass at the Monterey Bay Aquarium, then surfing monstrous waves in Oahu as a teen, then heaving through an Atlantic storm from the helm of his sailboat as a man in his thirties. Together, we have spent hours watching documentaries of famous surfers riding gigantic waves, and astrophysicists orgasming over black holes. Adam is a science geek and nature freak. He is my very hot, science geek, nature freak. And as much as I have supported the inner nerd in him, I do not want his obsession to literally whisk him away.

But I never tell my husband what to do, nor does he, me. We have made it this far in our freewheeling lives on our own, and then forged together, for this very reason. So, alone, I bound back into our home for safety, and trust my husband has good enough sense to not get himself killed.

The door to our apartment resists my pull, and then budges open. I scuttle into our bedroom and close the door behind me. Soon a steady, deafening, high-pitched whistling sound permeates the walls and my eardrums. Every few minutes, Irma slingshots stronger gusts at us, shaking the house, and violently rattling the doors in their frames.

Adam tumbles in, as though he has just dodged an oncoming train. He is laughing, panting, covered in rain.

"Holy shit!" he beams at me. "It's getting bad out there!" He throws on jeans, finally puts some shoes on, and then runs back out into our front room with the GoPro, struggling with the door on his way out.

"Please don't go outside anymore!" I shout, but he is gone.

I begin to notice a recurring fluctuation of pressure. At first, my ears plug and pop incessantly. Then my head feels like it may pop. Irma is playing tug of war with the bricks and mortar of our home, and the bones and muscles of our bodies. In an instant, she is guzzling up the atmosphere, swallowing gargantuan gulps of oxygen, trying her best to suck the walls from our home, the skulls from our brains. In the next instant, she is steamrolling us, shouldering against us with all of her indomitable might, trying to crush us. Adam runs in again once more, this time to stay.

"Is your head hurting?" he calls out.

"Yes," I cry, relieved to hear I am not experiencing this alone, ". . . like it's going to implode."

"Me too!" he commiserates and then pushes the bed firmly up against our bedroom door. We both jump in. I wonder how much worse it can get. How strong are her wind speeds now? She was predicted to reach 185 mph. What does that feel like? What if what we are experiencing now is only 150 mph, or 130 mph?

I dread to speculate that we may still be in Irma's infantile stage. That this may be only the beginning.

"I have to pee," I confess.

"Okay, go quickly."

Inside the bathroom, I pee as quickly as I can and then return to the bedroom. I decide not to flush, as our electricity is out. When the power is out, our water pump is disabled. No water will flow through the pipes, except for the water that sits in the pipes already. It could be awhile until we can flush again, and when we do, we will have to manually flush it, using water from our stockpile. I'd prefer to use our water reserve for drinking and washing, rather than flushing. I figure a stinky toilet is more tolerable than thirst.

Suddenly, we hear something upstairs.

"What is that?" I ask aloud, afraid to acknowledge the truth.

At first, it is breaking glass. Gradually the sounds grow deeper and louder, as though our neighbors are dragging their furniture across the floor and ramming it into the walls. But our upstairs neighbors vacated before the storm. That is Irma.

"Oh shit," Adam replies. "That's not good."

Irma has penetrated the second floor. We both know that once the wind has pierced a structure, it is likely that the place will soon be torn apart from the inside, as well as the outside. Somebody has let the big bad wolf in.

Like hiding in a house that's being burglarized, we lay petrified, hoping that Irma only ransacks the upstairs, and leaves the downstairs alone. The banging and bashing noises from overhead paint a grim scene in our imaginations of what may soon happen to us.

"Can we go in the bathroom? It doesn't hurt to be prepared. Let's just get in the tub and be ready." I plead with Adam. I recall my childhood years in Erie, having to hide in the basement when tornadoes approached. Tornadoes move fast and give very little warning of their arrival. I'm accustomed to retreating to the safest place in the home from the onset, and hunkering down until the funnel has passed. It makes sense to do that now, but Adam is resistant.

We lay on our bed, as Irma's rampage above us grows more violent, and her tremendous gusts more fiercely rattle our home and psyches.

"I'll be back," Adam utters and jumps from the bed. I move back into the bathroom to double-check its suitability as a last-resort bunker. Adam pulls the bed away from the door that leads from the bedroom to the front room. Again he struggles to pull open this door—this time he is almost unable, the pressure drop outside our home so severe. Finally, the door gives and Adam disappears. Moments later, he is back.

"It's time to go to the bathroom," he calmly but emphatically commands. I do not ask what he has seen that has suddenly changed his mind. I do not need to know, relieved and eager to follow his orders. Then Adam remembers he left his laptop on a chair pressed up against the wall in the front room. He tries to make a run for it, but this time cannot open the door. He pulls against it with all his might and body weight. Adam is a solid, muscular, 5-11 foot, 185 pound man and yet he is a paperweight in comparison to Irma's Goliath-like strength. Finally the door releases open during a lull in the sporadic gusts, and he dashes in and back out, laptop in hand.

We push the bed back up against the door, and take mere seconds to haul our heavy queen-sized mattress into our tiny bathroom, wedging it through the narrow door frame. Adam enters the floor of the shower first, laying atop our couch cushions which have been crammed to fit. I jam my body beside him, laying on my side, since there is not enough room for us to lay on our backs. The mattress is too large to squeeze neatly inside our shower (or our bathroom, for that matter), so we have to curl its long edges along our sides. Adam grabs the right side; I grab the left. He hands me a pillow.

"Put this over your face." I try to fix it firmly somehow between my face and the toilet, although I need one hand to hold down the mattress. I wish we had helmets. This pillow will blow away with a light breeze. And a strong breeze will smash this toilet straight into my face.

There are two doors that lead into this room—one leading to the bedroom that opens inward, and one leading to the kitchen that opens outward, the latter of which could pose a serious problem. At this point, we are still assuming that if the outer shell of our home is compromised, there will be things coming *in* at us. Nowhere did we read in any hurricane preparedness guide, that things may be sucked *out*.

While the pressure will suction the inward-opening door airtight—Irma would have to break the door jamb in order to bust through—the outward-opening door facing the kitchen and the seascape could easily be suctioned away.

Irma now seems to be in our home, her battle cry drowning out every other sound. We no longer hear furniture dragging around upstairs, only this shrieking blood-curdling roar, like a continuous symphony of subway trains in your skull.

I am afraid to move. Adam and I do not speak. I find it difficult to breathe, and we both sweat profusely. The smell of my own urine from the toilet makes me want to vomit. I try to breathe slowly, doing my best to stay calm, to stay sane.

The bathroom door begins convulsing, possessed by otherworldly forces. Adam finally confesses what he saw when he opened our bedroom door.

"Our front doors," he manages to utter, "they've been sucked away."

"They're open?!? The wind is coming straight in?!? What did you see!?!" Fear spews out of me like lava.

"I didn't want to tell you, but in case that bathroom door doesn't hold," his voice seems to trail off... "Just be ready..."

Now each time our flimsy wooden bathroom door thrashes around in the frame, I realize what is on the other side. Nothing. Nothing but those small kitchen drawers that Adam had the good judgment to leave a few inches ajar. And Irma's 185+ mph grisly force.

She yanks at the doorknob like a vicious giant with all her strength, trying to tear the door open. She pauses. We breathe. Ten seconds pass. She tries again, with more psychotic rage and brute strength—surely this time she will rip that door right off. We hold our breath and tighten our grip. She pauses. We breathe again for thirty seconds. And then she's at it again . . .

I don't want to die.

I wonder how long she will last. Harvey hovered over Houston for days. But Irma is moving faster. Maybe eight more hours? Maybe ten? I keep slipping in and out of consciousness, my mind apparently shutting down what it can, short-circuited and overloaded by this hailstorm of stimulation and terror. Or is it a lack of oxygen in the air? All the while, the muscles of my hand and forearm are flexed, gripping with full strength my side of the mattress, which very well could be what ends up saving our lives.

A mattress. If a concrete wall cannot stop a 2X4 from shanking me, how the hell is this mattress going to? And once the winds rip through here, how can I possibly hold this mattress down? I am not as strong as Adam. What if I let go and expose both of us to the elements? Maybe I can wrap my leg around the mattress. How long could my leg endure a barrage of flying debris before it releases?

I have a good knowledge of human anatomy. I picture nails, hinges, wooden beams, scraps of metal ripping through my jeans into the flesh of my leg, cutting through layers of tissue, then hitting the bone, shredding the leg into pieces. I know the muscle is deep, and the hamstring (holding this death grip on this mattress) is in the back of the leg, so as long as I can protect my hamstring curled around this mattress from being severed, and can endure the pain and the horror of feeling the front of my leg cleaved apart, I think I could hang on for at least thirty minutes.

I try to turn my face away from the demonic shimmying door, and the toilet, which as the hours pass, begins to look more and more like a porcelain battering ram.

I don't want to die.

Irma's banshee cry is deafening. Her gusts ram us in terrifying waves that feel as though the entire house will be ripped away, like our skulls will be sucked from our bodies. Every tortuous blast of wind cuts straight through to my soul. My heart sputters, my mind lobotomized by sheer terror, this agony of helplessness and vulnerability unlike anything I have ever known.

I think of people who spend their lives hiding. Refugees, stowaways, runaway slaves, Anne Frank. How did that poor little girl do it? For years... What we have to endure before we can even remotely understand extreme human suffering. [Strangely, I will later meet another Irma survivor, a Tortolan, who also thought of Anne Frank during this time.]

I pass out again.

Another ghastly gust and terrible suction in my head jolts my eyes open. I peer up at the small window above Adam's head, and pray that a mudslide does not come to smother us. Or that the window does not break and slice my husband to pieces.

It is best to prepare myself for the worst, I tell myself. So what will that be? Be ready for it, because it may be happening, any moment now. And then you can at least comfort yourself: "Well, you always knew this might happen."

I envision the bathroom door sucking away, and the roof bursting into the air like an exploding piñata. I imagine the mattress being ripped from my grip and my body flung into a draft, a steel beam impaling me straight through my abdomen, splicing my internal organs—I am a goner now—and Irma fastball pitching me up against the mountain side, where hopefully I am knocked unconscious by the impact, before I bleed to death slowly.

The wind gradually tapers down to an eerie silence.

"Is it the eye?" Adam says and pries himself from our sweaty, stinky bunker. I stay behind. "Holy shit," Adam calls to me. "You need to see this." I follow him tepidly, afraid to see what Irma has done. From the bathroom to the bedroom (so far so good) to our front room, where the ghostly gray sky looms through what once were our french doors . . .

We stand aghast. The doors are gone. Our armoire has been bisected—one half of it gone, the other half bashed to pieces and strewn along our balcony and hillside below. Our couch is lacerated, as though a lunatic slashed it for hours with a machete, and lays smashed and flipped against the bathroom door, along with everything else in the room. Grass and leaves coat the ceiling and walls, a layer of rainwater coats our floor. This "room" is unrecognizable.

The wind still lingers outside, a subdued but potent presence, enough to deter me from immediately following

Adam out onto the balcony. I just know everybody is dead. I am not ready to look out, to see the carnage of our beautiful Cane Garden Bay community.

Through the gaping hole of our living room, now a gruesome eye forced open to unimaginable destruction, Adam crouches over a lit cigarette. The sky forebodes, Irma is just giving us a "breather."

My body begins trembling, then shakes uncontrollably. I barely make it to the balcony before I am puking over the edge, presumably from the cortisol riveting through my system. Adam begins filming the landscape. I hear our neighbor and turn to see the dividing wall between our porches is gone. But he is alive.

"Are you guys okay?!" Adam calls to him.

"Yes, we are okay!"

We scan right and left, and for the first time can see every home, every shop, every bar. All the trees are severed. What normally is a thick canopy of gloriously green vegetation veiling and providing privacy to each residence, is now a wasteland of dead jagged stumps. We see huge slabs of houses splattered about, cars overturned and lodged in the mountainside. There is a mass of overturned boats slammed together in the swirling bay, now devoid of wind with the wall of Irma's eye miles away. We keep looking for people. Where are the people?

Then we see the house below us, a two-story, the roof gone, the first floor ceiling gone. We gaze directly down into the first-floor bedroom, but we cannot see any people. Whoever lived here, I pray he or she is alive.

"I hope this isn't just the eye?" Adam warns our neighbor, who seems surprised to hear this. How many people on Tortola know? Collectively, we all have only a short window of respite before the second half of Irma bears down on us. And the wall of the eye will be her strongest blow. I pray that people understand this.

Adam goes around the side of the house to pee, and I do the same, squatting in the open dank air. When we return to the balcony, we witness a few people starting to appear from the wreckage. From a distance, we wave to each other.

Adam shouts, "This is just the eye!" They squint back, seemingly in confusion.

"This is just the eye! We are only halfway through! Get ready!!" he calls again.

"Is your place still safe?" I ask our neighbor. "Do you feel safe to stay there for the second half?"

He tells us his place is okay—no broken windows or missing doors...yet. Looking over my shoulder at the skeleton of our own home, I dare to ask if we can stay with him. But he has a family of three, and there is certainly no room for us in his shower, so I hold my tongue. The thought of climbing back into our shower and enduring another four or five hours of hell is mind-numbing, especially now that we have confirmation: the outer armor of our home is gone. I glance in at that feeble, hollow bathroom door. We are about to enter battle with THAT as our shield.

Adam predicts that the second half of the storm will hit with winds from the south, on our neighbor's side, and he warns him of that. I feel sick thinking about the three of them hiding in their shower with their beautiful little boy. Our neighbor begins boarding up his front French doors, when he sees what has happened to ours. I try to light a cigarette, but keep dropping it, my hands still shaky. Finally, I light one, and gasp in sweet gulps of nicotine.

Gawking at the desolation below our balcony, every window and door in every house now a dark vacuous hole, every roof chipped away, I struggle to find a single structure that stands unscathed. On her first tour of Cane Garden Bay, Irma had paid everyone a visit, even the mansions towering high on the ridge, which surely must have been hurricane-proof fortified with fortunes only the island's wealthiest could afford. No amount of power or prestige, no particular faith, no right connection, no family ties could have spared anyone from Irma. Dizzied by the evidence before our eyes, the incomprehensibly ugly aftermath of her passage, we are wising up to what it will take the meteorologists, journalists, the world, weeks to figure out: Irma is in a class of her own.

I cannot fathom how these homes will endure another

several hours of battery, nor how the island will ever recover. We will need power, and money, and connections, and faith to restore the BVI.

"At least we have Richard Branson," I mutter dazedly. "He loves the BVI. This is his home. He will help rebuild and bring attention and aid to the island. And he has the power, the intelligence…the money to do it."

We also now see how unprotected we were on our northernmost side from Irma's first round of fury. The typically lush landscape made it impossible for us to gauge the distance between us and the nearest structure, which we now see is actually quite far. Irma had plenty of ground to get a running start before she slammed up against us, and the formerly dense mass of trees did nothing to slow her down.

"The second half should not be as bad for us—she'll be coming from the south," Adam assures me, "but let's start preparing." He runs out to the car to see if he can pick up a weather update on the radio, with no luck. On his way, he notices that our upstairs neighbors must have left a window open, which would explain how Irma's tentacles managed to infiltrate. I salvage what I can from our front room—shoes, clothing, a few books—and toss them into the bedroom, hopeful that this room remains untouched.

When Adam returns, he takes the rope and loops it around the mattress like a belt, fastening a carabiner to each end, which will serve as handles for us to more securely clamp down the mattress. He then takes my resistance bands and ties them from the inside doorknob of our bathroom door to the towel rack.

After roughly 45 minutes, the wind begins to pick up. We take in one last breath of fresh air, one last view of the bay, and climb back into the shower stall.

Soon, the wall of the eye is upon us. The winds lunge at us like ferocious pent-up Rottweilers. Irma is even stronger this time around, but we are more protected this time. With tireless brutality, she tries to penetrate our inner sanctuary. Adam and I again lay in silence, gripping the mattress, sweating, barely breathing, while Irma tries to tear our home apart.

I'm not sure if I can handle any more of this. I think about all the times I have put my body and my health at risk before, in stupid reckless ways. What a luxury to have control over your own health and safety. I will surely never take such a gift for granted again.

Irma will not leave us alone. She smashes her fists against the walls unrelentingly and yanks at the roof. I do whatever I can to stay sane, my mind tormented. I try to think of something I can repeat to myself, like a mantra, something that will help calm me. Finally, it comes to me. Deep from the reservoir of my childhood memories of Catholic school days. A remnant from a more innocent, more hopeful, me. A me who always believed I was loved by, and a part of, something greater. That, at any moment, all I had to do was call out, and there was somebody, or something, there to listen.

The Hail Mary.

It's innocuous. It's soothing. And it's the only thing I can seem to remember by heart right now.

Hail Mary
Full of grace
The Lord is with thee.
Blessed art thou amongst women
And blessed is the fruit of thy womb Jesus.
Holy Mary
Mother of God
Pray for us sinners
Now and at the hour of our death,
Amen.

In my mind, I repeat. For four hours of horror. The Hail Mary rocks me in and out of consciousness, lulling me back and forth from my waking state to my dreams.

Adam and I are still and silent as corpses. Our heads throb and our ears feel as though someone is shoving giant rocks into them and then ripping them out, again and again. I begin to count the seconds in between the sustained 185 mph winds and those god-awful gusts of 200+ mph winds, as a quasi-scientific gauge of Irma's orientation.[7]

Of course, at the time, we do not realize that the barometric pressure is plunging to 914 mb, which is the equivalent of suddenly being catapulted over 3000 ft into the air (over twice the height of the Empire State Building). When atmospheric pressure drops drastically, as occurs in mountain-climbing, there is less air pumping into the lungs, less oxygen reaching the blood and organs, and symptoms of hypoxia onset—hence the drowsiness, shallow breath, and drop in blood pressure. But in mountain climbing, you ascend slowly, allowing your body time to adjust along the way.

I remember from hiking Kilimanjaro in 2013, the local Chagga tribesmen, hired as porters, admonishing over-ambitious hikers in Swahili: "Pole, pole!" or "Slow, slow!" I also remember a teenager not heeding their advice, racing to the climax of the mountain and severe hypoxia, only to jump from the edge—deranged by the lack of oxygen to his brain. (He survived, but had to be airlifted to a hospital.)

Irma now offers us no chance of a gradual modest acclimation to this drop in pressure. No "pole, pole" for us. If the terror of our predicament was not enough to make us feel deranged, hypoxia may do the trick.

After four grueling hours of cowering helplessly from Irma's psychotic rage, I count 300 seconds—so far, the longest span of moderate cessation—and I know she is leaving us. For a moment I grieve for whomever she meets next, whichever island, whichever family huddling in their bathtub fearing for their lives. My relief for myself is tainted

---

[7] The only observations of 200+ mph winds, clocked by land-based wind gauges, cannot be confirmed. Even NOAA's most recent official report notes the uncertainty of its estimate of Irma's 178 mph sustained winds due to disparity between readings by SFMR, and the Air Force Reserve and NOAA Hurricane Hunters. John P. Cangialosi, Andrew S. Latto, and Robbie Berg. "NATIONAL HURRICANE CENTER TROPICAL CYCLONE REPORT. HURRICANE IRMA." Page 5. 30 June 2018. https://www.nhc.noaa.gov/data/tcr/AL112017_Irma.pdf

with the realization that Irma has not just disappeared. She is merely on her way to more victims. Hail Mary, pray for them.

For the last time, Adam and I pry ourselves from the cramped confines of our shower and tread slowly, in case Irma has any more tricks up her sleeves, through the shambles of our home. [Later, we agree that if Irma had persisted even another hour longer, our chintzy bathroom door and punctured roof most likely would have gone. And if we hadn't passed through the eye, many of Tortola's inhabitants would have not had a chance to find more secure shelter or further fortify their broken homes.] Our bedroom floor is covered in several inches of water. Our front room is slathered with a fresh layer of nature. Even a small frog clings to our kitchen wall, its small heart beating in terror, having been flung from its hiding place faraway. The scraps of our furniture and belongings have been whirled and slung all around in chaos.

Adam and I again assume everybody is dead. Dumbfounded by our own survival, feeling like we narrowly escaped demise, we cannot imagine, or rationalize, why or how. To ask for more seems greedy or foolish. To extend that disbelief, to hope that others were as freakishly lucky, is beyond where my bludgeoned heart, and drubbed brain, have the stamina to venture.

To this day, I am still unable to adequately express the depth of my anguish at this very moment, this stretch of time where I thought that everybody I loved, every neighbor, every friend in my beloved Tortola, was dead. It is a feeling I wish no one ever has to experience.

Outside, the once benign Caribbean sea has swallowed and spit out 100 meters of oceanfront. Brown miry water pools inland, over the waterfront road, and up the low hillside to the community center, dredging chunks of mystery matter, which bob and disappear below the surface. This center was another "emergency shelter" recommended by the BVI Department of Disaster Management (DDM). Its roof half-blown off, the Cane Garden Bay Community Center is now surrounded by water, any possible survivors marooned within a moat of filth. My heart heaves with shock and gratitude when a few survivors begin to stagger out and courageously wade through the water. They are presumably going to look for others.

As predicted by my brother David, the biggest structures, namely churches and community centers like this one (ironically designated as emergency shelters), ended up worse hit, their expansive roofs effortlessly picked and drop-kicked by Irma. I am glad we did not choose to stay there.

Soon our next-door neighbor steps out onto his balcony. We greet each other with spontaneous smiles and tears in our eyes. He tells us his apartment miraculously stayed intact, protected by a retaining wall and the hillside. His 3-year-old son apparently slept through the entire thing. We laugh with deep uncontrollable giddiness and gratitude.

The houses in our view have been further dismantled— more windows, doors, walls, or entire roofs missing. To our left, a car has rolled to a crashing stop against a stone wall, left flattened on its side. We debate whether or not to forage down the road, but the wind still undulates with unexpected force. Even our walk to the driveway seems brazen, as gusts threaten to hurtle us into the air. We notice Zorro had been pushed six feet and somehow stopped inches away from smashing our neighbor's SUV. I count another blessing.

We check on our upstairs neighbors' apartment, which was rendered fully transparent by Irma's redecorating touches. The roof above their bedroom and bathroom has peeled away, the ceiling collapsed in some areas, with a mixture of roofing materials, sunlight and rain dumping down into their apartment. Five inches of floodwater swishes broken bits of their home and personal possessions throughout their apartment. I instinctually climb in over shattered glass and begin rescuing their belongings from the water and placing them on counter tops and shelves. But the sodden sky blackens with nightfall, and we are running out of time to prepare our own home for an evening of darkness and exposure to the elements.

As I struggle back through their door frame, gripping the jambs to lift myself over the mess, I halt suddenly to avoid gouging my eye on a triangular door hinge that has been slung and lodged like a ninja star in their armoire. I shudder to think what that could have done to a human skull.

Back downstairs in our place, Adam and I clear a path through our front room to the balcony, pushing large broken pieces of furniture to the side. We light a few candles and Adam pulls meat from the freezer to cook on the grill, which somehow survived. I pick up our own remaining possessions, now saturated, and sweep flood water and debris out and off our balcony. Normally I would never throw debris, not even a paperclip, into the greenery below, but now there is no greenery, and there is debris everywhere.

We drag two chairs out onto the balcony where we eat our beans and meat, grateful to be able to cook on our gas stove and grill. As we quietly sip warm beers and chain-smoke, we scan for signals of distress from our Cane Garden Bay community. A few car alarms rant from afar, but eventually cease. Then we spot a light from up on a hill flashing with disconcerting regularity. Is someone asking for help? What if someone is trapped, or in need of medical care? Soon, that too, ceases.

Cortisol still courses through me, an elixir of elation and shock. There is not enough beer in the world to tranquilize me, not enough nicotine to reign in my feral nerves. I still cannot believe we are alive. I hope others were so lucky.

Our bodies eventually beg to break down, and our hearts and minds finally grant them permission. Adam and I retrieve our mattress from the shower and drag the bed-frame away from the door, to transform our bed back from a barricade into a place of repose. We surrender to, perhaps, one of the deepest sleeps of our lives.

CHAPTER 6: TEAM HUMANITY

Stirred by the sun, we arise on Thursday, September 7th, around 6 a.m., eager to get down the hill as soon as possible to see what remains of our community, where we can help, possibly catch a cellular signal to communicate with family back home, and get information. I make us egg sandwiches and coffee. From our balcony, we immediately sense something is missing—there is not a single bird or tree frog or chicken to be seen or heard, our normal soundtrack of animal chatter now muted to a sickening silence. We spot a few of our friends on the road below us. They say they are heading down the mountain to see who needs help. We tell them we are following.

Our neighbor attempts to drive his car down but is halted by a fallen tree entangled in electrical lines blocking the road. He leaves his car there. Adam and I climb over, careful not to touch the wires, even though the power was cut island-wide many hours ago. At the bottom of the hill, our fears are realized. The damage we observed from a distance is worse than we could have imagined. Not a single beachfront bar, home or restaurant was spared, some buildings sundered, others completely gone or shoved, like Glenn's convenient store, fifty feet inland. Flipped forty-foot cargo containers, planks of wood (scaffolding from the half-built Quitos hotel), steel beams, crushed cars and boats, and massive mangled trees clutter the roads, which are half gone, covered in sand and rubble. Debris is everywhere. And yet every person we pass is a cause for celebration. How did everyone survive?

I am high on gratitude, each human I see a miracle, a statistical oddity, a feat of perseverance, a testament to humanity. "Glad you're okay," each of us beams to the other. Many rummage through the wreckage and try to locate their possessions that Irma flushed away, or scavenge for necessities to replace what they have lost. Adam and I decide to keep our eyes peeled for a bucket to haul water from our cistern if need be.

We see our typically jocose South African friend Jason, standing motionless along the roadside, stunned to stillness, his usually bright eyes and cheerful smile paralyzed by grief. Like us, he loves Cane Garden Bay and is known to regularly remark, "Man, it doesn't get much better than this, does it?" He lives with his wife and two small children in the same building as our friend Kay, who is housing Murray, the sailor whose unfortunate boat delivery landed him here.

"The destruction is just… And Jose is next, I can't, I can't believe this…" he rambles and gazes vapidly, as though conversing with a ghost.

I ask him, "Where is Kay? Is she okay? Where is she?"

"Everything is gone. Everything. Everything is gone," he repeats.

I ask again, "Have you seen Kay? Is she okay?"

He only repeats himself more emphatically. "*Everything is gone.*"

I interpret this to mean that Kay is dead. I step back and take a moment to digest this. I tell myself to face reality. There will only be more news like this—I expected this. But how can I not be riveted with despair? I feel sick. No no. This can't be true. I decide to ask one more time, and then I will swallow this truth. Jason maunders on, "It's just all gone. Everything…"

"Where is KAY!?" I jolt him into making eye contact with me.

"Kay is somewhere along the beach. She's okay. I just saw her . . ."

I break away and head towards the beach. I don't see her, but I do see many others. Each face throttles me with joy like I have never felt before. Humans. How did we all survive? Irma was so much stronger than us. She should have killed us, every one. I cannot imagine anything perhaps more uniting, more bonding for the human race, than having to survive against a common assailant with the magnitude, the dominance, of Irma.

I continually check my phone for reception, but no luck. I worry for my family. The stress I imagine they feel compounds my own, and I cannot do anything else now but find a way to reach them and let them know we are okay. We decide to walk east where I spot a swarm of people gathering near a jumble of boat fragments smashed against the rocks. Finally I see Kay and Murray. We all hug—even Murray, no longer a stranger in this place. We are all family now, Team Humanity.

They share their own survival tale, far more harrowing than our own. The nightmarish fate we had dreaded befell them when their entire roof blew off from over their heads. They fled to an outdoor concrete storage room during the eye, salvaged doors from the house to seal off the enclosure, and for the duration of the second half of the storm, they sat with their backs against that door, their legs against a wall, pushing for their lives to keep Irma from sucking it, and them, away.

Holding up my phone like a beacon, I see others precariously climb out onto the rocks, so I follow, trying not to slip or drop the phone. Finally I pick up an AT&T signal from neighboring St. Thomas, which we can see in the distance. I send a text to my mom, my brothers, and my best friend Kate back in the states:

"Are you there? We are alive."

I am able to call my mom who answers frantically: "Diandra! Oh my God, are you there? You're alive. Thank God." The reception is spotty and gaps of silence snatch away her words.

"Mom?!? MOM?!?" The others on the rocks nearby crowd closer when they hear me talking, and try to catch the signal for themselves.

"Diandra?! Are you there? Can you hear me??"

"The call keeps breaking up. Now I can hear you..." There is a small crowd of people gathered around me, desperate for an update, my mom now a lifeline for us all.

"I've been worried sick. Trying to reach you. We all have . . ." She breaks into tears. My own eyes water, but there are more pressing matters.

"We're alive mom. Please get in touch with Adam's mom to let her know. Half of our home was destroyed, but the bedroom and bathroom are in tact. We can stay there. My car also survived. We have enough food and water for a week. I love you. I'm going to hang up to save my credit [mobile phone minutes] and my battery. I had to climb on the rocks to get a signal—I'll try to call you again tomorrow, if I can catch a signal. I love you."

I am not sure if she has heard all of what I have said, but I can tell she hesitates to say goodbye, still crying. I take comfort knowing she will alert the rest of my family, and that she at least knows her daughter and her son-in-law are alive.

"Diandra, wait!" she shouts as if protecting me from an oncoming speeding car, "I almost forgot to remind you, Hurricane Jose is right behind Irma . . ." My breath stops. *One thing at a time*, I tell myself.

"Do you know when? How strong?" I ask.

"I don't know for sure, but I'll let you know as I hear.... I love you."

"Love you too, Mama. Good bye."

When I hang up, I relay to the others that Jose is still on its way, but we don't yet know his strength or date of arrival. They begin asking questions I cannot answer. I hope my family can.

I message my brother Darren in Chicago. He has always been my "go-to" for emergency situations, not that I've ever been in an emergency quite like this one before. He is the one I trust to act calmly and efficiently in high-stress situations, the problem solver, the engineer.

I text: "What is it like in STT [St. Thomas]? What are

the best odds of getting out of here? Evacuation plans for the BVI? More updates on Jose please. Only our bathroom and bedroom are in tact. Our roof is coming off. Not sure we can take Jose."

I don't hear back. I did not know at the time, but Darren had written me back immediately with updates on Jose, and possible relief efforts. The messages failed to reach us.

I decide to add, "We have no access to news and getting mixed messages. Just told Jose was coming tomorrow and was category-2. Check NOAA website was most accurate. Please keep sending updates. News updates on BVI? Everybody here is completely helpless and uninformed. Trying to make it down the hill to get reception once a day. SURROUNDED BY GROUP OF PEOPLE ASKING QUESTIONS. When is BVI airport open FERRIES running? Need info."

I send messages per request on behalf of friends, and lend my phone to a few others, to notify families abroad that we are all okay. Our dear friend Kate calls us from Washington, D.C. She too cries and is so thankful we are alive.

"Everything is destroyed, Kate." She was my neighbor in the U.S. Virgin Islands, where we both lived for three years. She knows the beauty of these islands and feels this loss personally.

"The destruction is horrific," I add, "you wouldn't recognize it…"

"Diandra," she summons her inner pragmatism, "It's going to be at least a year until the island will recover. You guys may need to get out of there…" Suddenly, the sky cracks open and pelts us with an onslaught of freezing cold hail. Everyone within range races to a nearby tipped container for shelter.

"I have to run Kate! I think it's hailing!" It is the first time I have seen or heard of hail in the Caribbean.

In those few moments huddling together under the container, we all question whether we had strayed too early from the safety of our homes.

Has Irma turned around? Could it be Jose already? Thankfully, the hail subsides, but it's enough to inspire Adam and me to gather whatever more we need from the bay, and then get back home.

Just then a young woman holding a baby, and a middle-aged woman pass by. Their faces reveal weariness and despair.

"Do you need to use my phone?" I ask.

"Yes. Yes, please. Thank you." The young woman hands her baby to whom must be the grandmother, and sends a few messages from the rocks. Once finished, she passes me the phone, thanks me again, and the grandmother explodes into fervent Spanish, as she returns the infant to his mother's arms. I assume they are from the Dominican Republic, which is where the majority of Tortola's Spanish-speaking population hails from. The young lady begins to translate what her mother is trying to tell me...

"The storm. It is so bad," she pauses. "We almost die. The wind? It pull the baby away. But I grabbed her, and my mother, she grabbed me. We hold, we hold, we hold..." She squints her eyes and wrinkles up her face, as her mother shakes her head and prays up to heaven.

"We alive. Thank God. We alive." She then tells me they had just walked three hours up and over the mountain from where they lived in Road Town, with hopes that Cane Garden Bay was in better shape. Their home was leveled. Anyone who knows Tortola's terrain, (studded with 1700 foot mountains that rise and plunge abruptly into the next, and only a minuscule percentage of the island actually flat), can attest what a grueling hike theirs must have been. I hope for their sake, Cane Garden Bay is in "better shape," although I cannot comprehend how that could be true.

They drift along down the road to join the horde of other roaming, dazed drifters. We decide while we are down here, we should try to find more drinking water. We start to leave again, when I see a tall, slender white-haired man whom I have never before seen, in pressed slacks and a bright white linen shirt, slumped and seated on the seawall, all alone. He is staring blankly, his thin brown arms folded across his lap. I approach him and decide to offer him my phone as well.

"Excuse me, do you need to use a phone?"

His face brightens as he looks at us. "Oh yes, please! Oh thank you! My name is Clem."

"Hi, I'm Diandra. This is my husband Adam."

"I would just like to call my daughter in Philadelphia, if that's all right. I will not talk long. Just to let her know I am okay. I know she must be very worried."

"Of course!" we respond.

He makes his call quickly and hands us back the phone, as he overflows in gratitude. "Thank you, thank you again," and he begins to take a seat back on the wall. His eyes are still glassy with sorrow and his broad thin shoulders slouch with bereavement.

"Excuse me, but do you live here? Do you have someplace to stay?"

"Oh, it's kind of you to ask," he responds. "This is not my home. I'm from Philly. I'm just here on vacation. I'm staying there," he points at Quito's now tattered guesthouse up the road, "and my room is livable. I can stay there."

"Do you need anything?"

"Well, I'm a little concerned, because, you see, I have only credit cards. I have only a little cash." His gaze is distant, his speech hurried, as though his thoughts and words are trying to flee from his agitated body, which is stuck here, on an island full of strangers, far from his family, amidst one of the greatest natural disasters in recent history. I sense that Clem is normally a responsible man, who does not readily walk himself into precarious situations.

"I don't have much food and water, since I'm only here on vacation. But I should be okay for the next few days. I feel better at least now that I've been able to speak with my daughter. She was so worried. So thank you."

Without hesitation, Adam and I promise to return the next day with water and food for him. He insists we don't need to, and we insist we do.

Now we too drift in shock back up the road, digging up a couple buckets from the debris along the way. A small crew of men from the community drag a bloated goat carcass, apparently drowned, across the road and to the beach. One man jokes and invites us to an evening beach barbecue. Our mind turns to Tanner and Victor and we decide to turn up a side-road where resides one local family who has regularly fed them. Sickened with dread, we scan the now swampy perimeters of the road for their bodies, daring not to believe they may have somehow survived. Another mob of older, long-standing Cane Garden Bay patriarchs, a few of them already drunk off rum, are laying wooden planks across an umber pool of floodwater to create a pathway to a fully-stocked rum shack that survived amidst the wreckage.

Just then we see Victor. He is swollen, bruised and tattooed with lesions around his head and body, but he is alive. He does not come to us, but staggers past in an apparent daze. Imagining what terrible trauma Victor may have incurred, having had to possibly tread for hours through turbulent swell, being gashed by debris in the air and in the water, we beckon him, longing to care for him. As though he does not even recognize us, or perhaps he cannot see us, he staggers past us and is gone.

Next we see Tanner. He is trotting behind one of the local men, the owner of the bar, who often feeds him. Adam and I shout his name, "Tanner!" and his tail immediately beats rapidly behind his perfectly intact body as he looks up at us. He starts to approach, when the bar owner cheerfully explains, "This little guy came in with me just before the storm. He was smart." Tanner stays close to the heels of his protector and follows the grandfathers of Cane Garden Bay into the bar to celebrate their survival. We let him be, satisfied that he is alive and in good hands, and continue back down the road.

Each friend we pass is a conversation, a hug, a cry, a harrowing story, a warning, bits of hearsay about how the rest of the island has fared and updates on oncoming Jose. The walk alone down this half-mile stretch of village road is emotionally exhausting. We hear Road Town is in shambles, that the newly built cruise ship pier and all of its quaint boutiques have been blown to smithereens. We hear a 64-

foot 45 ton plus catamaran was uprooted and lobbed atop a guard station at Nanny Cay Marina. We hear some areas of the island have slid into chaos, looting, crime, violence. Most poignantly, we hear of no deaths, though surely, there must be some.

Somebody relays that there will be a town meeting at the Methodist Church sometime the following day.

Our friend Vanicia passes us with her eight-year-old son, both struggling over the debris in raincoats and boots. She is looking for a cellular signal. After exchanging any information we have gathered, we ask how she and her son handled the storm. She tells us that at one point, they were climbing into their "safe room" when the wind suddenly swung the door shut behind her and trapped her son on the outside. He was screaming for her and she was unable to open the door due to the suction of the wind. She shouted to him, "KICK! KICK DOWN THE DOOR!" The little boy kicked and kicked and finally bust it open to be with his mom.

We reach our normal stop, Bobby's Market, only to find it badly damaged and boarded up, so we continue on towards Columbus Variety Store, a quarter-mile down the road. Passing the cemetery on the oceanside, I shiver to think what the flooding may have done to the grave-sites.

Columbus is destroyed. The kind young cashier who always smiles sullenly hauls packages of food and water from the heap of refuse (that once was their family store) up and over a broken wall, and stacks them along the perimeter. I dawdle awkwardly on the road, sensing the gravity of their loss, unsure whether they would welcome business at such a time, or whether they prefer to pick up the pieces of their family legacy without disturbance. Our personal misfortune feels trivial. Adam and I lost our apartment where we've lived for one year. This family has lost their business that they've built over generations.

At the very least, I decide to greet him. "Glad you are okay, and I'm sorry about the destruction to your store." His familiar smile returns as he looks up at us.

"Please, I don't mean to impose, but could we purchase

water? I have cash. We don't mind paying more… If now is not a good time, we understand, of course."

He gazes around and I can painfully see that he wants to help us, but the task is daunting. His mother overhears from inside their house and steps out. "Yes, that's okay. We will find some…" she says and nods to her son.

The young man roots around and finds a pile of one-liter water bottles buried deep below mounds of spoiling produce.

"How many?" he calls out.

"How about ten dollars worth?" I decide quickly, trying to recall exactly how much drinkable water we have at home, how long we may have to subside, and how much cash we have left.

He digs out three 1.5 liter bottles and gives us back two dollars in change. I feel badly that he has charged us so little.

"Thank you," I say. "Good night," and we head home. I pray that he clears up the mess quickly, before sunset, or at least before people start to get desperate. I worry that all of that unprotected merchandise has rendered him and his family vulnerable to looting.

In the middle of the night, Adam and I wake to rustling in the front room. Our own home with its doors and windows punched out is now a wide open invitation to anyone or anything.

"What is that?" I whisper as I sit up in bed. "Adam, do you hear that?"

We listen and try to quiet our breath and still our movement. We hear it again, a scratching then a scurrying sound.

"It must be an animal," Adam concludes, listening a little longer to be proven wrong. "Yeah, it's just an animal. It must be looking for food. Let it look, there's nothing to find…"

PART II: IRMAGEDDON

CHAPTER 7: TWO DAYS AFTER IRMA

Anyone who has ever suffered the type of destruction caused by a cataclysmic hurricane will probably find the following chapters unremarkable. For the majority of the population who have not, you may find these events unbelievable, these thoughts unreasonable, these actions unjustifiable. Please know, my hardship now as I recount this time is to not understate its severity. After averting disaster, after surviving and realizing in hindsight, "Everything ended up working out," it is easy to trivialize, or undermine the true horror of the situation we suddenly all found ourselves in. Perhaps more challenging to accurately depict are moments, even private moments, of which we may not be proud. However, therein lie the deepest wounds inflicted by Irma, the damage not measurable in wind velocity or millibars of atmospheric pressure, or in layers stripped from your home, but rather, in layers stripped from your heart.

As I write seven months later from a posh coffee shop in downtown D.C., one of the many random cities to which we've been displaced since Irma, it is difficult for me to mentally and physically place myself back there. Finally, thankfully, the symptoms of post traumatic stress have faded. The nightmares of calamity; the irrational sensitivity to loud sounds, strong winds, any remotely far-reaching life-endangering encounter; even the profuse hippie-like love I felt for complete strangers in the ensuing months of Irma—all have gradually and subtly receded from my day-to-day life.

And now, back to "normal," I struggle to describe what it was like to be in one of the most abnormal situations human beings can find themselves.

In reality, there is no catchall hurricane survival guide or crucial token of wisdom any hurricane survivor can impart, including myself. Every hurricane is unique in its deadly concoction of virulence and destruction. The winds alone are entirely unpredictable, as we witnessed with Irma, which was a gargantuan cyclone full of cyclones, her random strikes having sometimes taken out all the walls of a home, while leaving a ceramic vase perfectly upright in its original position. Likewise, every hurricane-stricken terrain bears its own distinct advantages and disadvantages.

One glaringly obvious disadvantage of being on an island during a hurricane is its complete isolation from the outside world. It is not easy to leave beforehand, and nearly impossible after. If airports and ports are destroyed, as well as boats, ferries, even planes, as was the case in many of the islands hit by the hurricanes of 2017, not only can victims not escape, but aid workers and supplies cannot enter. When cellular towers and electrical grids are wiped out, there are no means of communication—either for status updates of situations on the ground, or for updates on the outside world, ensuing hurricanes, relief efforts, evacuation plans, etc. What the island man had taken centuries to mold into a port and a home, Irma had transformed back into to a remote, uninhabitable rock, in a matter of hours.

On a mountainous island like Tortola, if roads and vehicles are demolished, not only are residents cut off from the outside world, but they are also cut off from other areas of the island due to the steep imposing hills that divide one bay from the next. Unless you are healthy, brave and motivated enough to hike from one bay to the next, which requires energy and (consequently) water intake, and many people *were* and *did*, you are trapped where you are. That feeling of being held captive inside our shower, which had temporarily vanished along with the immediate threat of Irma, would soon be heightened to a new level. Soon we would be scanning the sea for boats, *any* boats, to take us away, and hoping we have enough cash or food to barter for an exodus.

One of the advantages of being in a small village on a small island, like Cane Garden Bay, in such a time is the close-knit nature of the community. Crime is virtually nonexistent, everybody knows everybody, and wrongdoers are easily and swiftly held accountable. Still Adam and I are caught off guard when, a couple days after Irma, we pass a notorious village "outlaw" storming down the road with a crew of followers like they're about to execute a heist. Last we heard, he was in jail.

And while I had assumed that the outside world knew how bad it must be, how desperate things were about to become, I did not learn something important until much later. In extreme hurricanes, most weather sensors on which news agencies and meteorologists rely on to gauge the severity, are destroyed by winds before the hurricane ever reaches its destination, or its maximum intensity. So, unbeknownst to us at the time, the outside world still has only a dim idea of the damage. If we had known this, we would have spent less time trying to "downplay the situation" to my family, thinking we were trying to keep them calm and better empower them to help us, and would have been blunt from the get-go, "We need help. All of us. We need help now."

Adam and I awake on Friday, September 8th, and immediately decide to tally how much food and water we have. We are fortunate to have a full cistern in our apartment, which we can use to wash ourselves and our dishes. As long as we have gas in our stove, we can boil that water for drinking and cooking. Adam points out that since all the gutters were destroyed, probably across island, once people's cisterns are empty, they can no longer be replenished by rainwater, so we need to conserve, not just for our own sake, but in case we need to share with others.

We have four full gallons of store-bought water, plus three remaining 1.5 liter bottles of water (thanks to Columbus Variety Store). We have a little meat in the fridge that needs to be eaten within the next few days. We have twelve cans of beans and soup, a large bag of chips, ten eggs, half a loaf of bread, and a few containers of Ramen noodles.

Our apartment needs attention. Not just because it's a depressing sight, but because it's unhygienic and is starting to stink of mold. Adam assumes the more labour-intensive duty of clearing heavy debris from our yard and the hill below our balcony. I do not envy him and am grateful for his muscularity in this arduous cleanup. He has to sift through mounds of heavy fractured tree limbs, roofing slates, splintered lumber, shards of broken glass, and countless scraps of our furniture and belongings scattered as far as we can see. I ask him to keep a lookout out for my guitar, which, with shameful sentimentality, I would like to see again. I am not so foolish as to think I will actually be able to strum her.

We have to be careful not to step on or grab anything that may hurt us, which is more challenging than one might imagine, when every object you encounter, every wobbly jagged Jenga tower of randomly piled debris we teeter on, is studded with nails or impaled with sharp projectiles. I imagine the hospital in Road Town, if it still stands, is not only difficult to get to, but is probably overloaded, under-resourced and understaffed. If worst comes to worst, we have the sewing kit in out bathroom cabinet, and Adam's handy pre-med training.

A safe distance from any houses, Adam has started a pile of trash to burn later, to which we make trips back and forth from the house carrying whatever cannot be salvaged. The sun scorches us so we walk slowly so as not to overexert ourselves and require too much drinking water. I neatly lay out along our porch any books and papers that may be salvageable. The flood water on our floor has mysteriously reappeared, and so I spend another hour sweeping. The work ahead of us seems endless, and as driven as we are to finish the task, we deem it more important to head back down the hill to catch the purported town meeting.

Impressively, the massive fallen tree and electrical wires that blocked our road have already been cleared by, we learn later, our ambitious neighbor. Adam and I feel guilty that we did not know to help, but with the threat of Jose nearing the island, we feel justified in prioritizing the cleanup and securing of our own home against another possible hit. With us we carry the large bag of chips and a 1.5 liter of water for Clem. In hindsight, this offering seems shamefully meager, but at the time, I felt like we were giving away our last dollar.

The barrage of faces and information and more stories of survival floods our hearts again. There are more residents wandering the road, and surprisingly, less wreckage. An excavator busily clears the road and we hear it is now possible to drive to Road Town, but not to Ballast Bay or Carrot Bay, immediately southwest of us. We first pass by the Methodist Church where a crowd gathers, but are told the meeting has not yet started, so we take this opportunity to try to get a signal to make a call.

"Diandra! Oh my God, Diandra!" It is our Canadian upstairs-neighbor and friend, Leah. Her face streaked with dirt, sweat and tears, she runs towards me and throws her arms around me.

"Oh my God! I thought you might be dead!" She weeps and I fight tears from invading my eyes, determined to stay in survival mode. "I thought all of Cane Garden Bay had to be wiped out. Our place, that huge fucking mansion I thought would be safer, was destroyed. Oh my God!" her words interrupted by sobs, "Oh my God, I'm so glad you're alive."

"I'm glad you're alive too!" I finally bellow back, allowing myself to feel comforted in this moment of emotional reckoning dear Leah has provided me. She takes a break from hugging me to squeeze Adam and wipe away her tears. I can see Adam feels momentary relief as well; a small smile of surprise brightens his face.

"Our building lost doors and windows, but it's still standing. We're okay! I'm glad you are too, Leah!" I echo her sentiment.

She grabs me again and pulls me close in another embrace. "Oh my God," she cries, her raw sweet emotion heartrending. She tells me they walked here from Zion Hill, a good seven kilometer trek up and over a few formidable bluffs. They are walking all the way to Road Town, checking on their friends in each community along the way. I commend her spirit, but wonder where they are staying for Jose.

"We have someplace safe to stay. Are you staying here? Don't be stupid. Don't stay here! You should stay with us," she berates us, alarming even herself.

"We will be okay. If we need to move someplace else, we will."

"I'm sorry. I know you're smart. You'll be okay. I'm just so happy you're alive."

"We haven't even looked into your place yet," I tell her.

"Oh shit, don't worry about it. There's nothing in there I care about. Just glad everybody's alive. I can't fucking believe this." She pulls the hair away from her face with both hands and looks around at the annihilation of Cane Garden Bay.

Peering down the road towards yesterday's AT&T "hotspot," I am discouraged by the absence of people on the rocks. I hug Leah and say goodbye as Adam and I tread towards the water's edge. When we reach, I know why the rocks are vacant. The AT&T signal can no longer be found. For twenty minutes, I hop from rock to rock, perch on my tiptoes with my phone suspended high above my head, futilely trying to bask in the rays of a cellular tower somewhere. I try to send a few texts to my family members, hoping that at least one may magically travel the distance, but my efforts are useless. Adam guides me to ask about relief efforts. We consider driving into town, but we still are not sure if the trip, and gas consumption, are necessary or even useful. What can Road Town offer if people have hiked for hours to find refuge here? I imagine there are no flights, no ferries, no grocery stores open, and possibly more desperation and crime than here. What if the car breaks down, as Zorro was prone to do, even in pre-Irma days—

such is her temperamental island-car way.

Back at the Methodist Church we wait for news, good or bad. Any perspective on the island's predicament is welcomed. An older, burly, bald, longstanding community member calls us all to attention. He explains what we know already: communication is broken. News from Road Town, from the Governor and Premier, from the other villages, is trickling in at a snail's pace, and much of the reports are dubious, inaccurate, or conflicting. A tall slender girl, maybe 17-years-old, circulates the crowd with a notebook and pen. She is collecting everybody's names, ages, occupation, and types of skills that may be called upon to help restore and sustain Cane Garden Bay's community in the days (or months?) of uncertainty ahead. The man explains that they need to know who is currently staying in Cane Garden Bay so they can be looked after. More importantly, a curfew will be instated, and anyone coming in and out of the village will be closely monitored, for the safety of all.

I list "teacher" as my occupation, and an image of a dusty schoolyard flashes through my mind, similar to the schools in the village of Taborah where I used to live and teach in Ghana. Romantically, I prepare myself to jump back into that role and become a useful member of this immediate community, if we do indeed stay isolated from the rest of the island, the rest of the world. But another thought comes to mind. Doesn't this seem like an illogical leap? We don't have enough water, enough food to last everyone here another week. How can we suddenly become self-sustaining from scratch? We can build a makeshift school in a day, but not a makeshift garden and a well or a desalination plant to feed everyone and keep everyone hydrated for days on end. We need outside help, or we need to get out.

A handsome, young-faced man in a T-shirt and jeans pulls up alongside the church and steps out of his car. I do not recognize him, but somebody tells me he is our district representative, the Honourable Melvin M. Turnbull. He shakes several people's hands, indiscreetly wipes a brow, furrowed with worry and responsibility and helplessness, and speaks quietly into the ear of our community leader. The community members murmur to one another, passing along hugs and greetings, pleased to see one another standing.

The Methodist Church is offered to everyone as a shelter and a community center for information, food, supplies, medical care, etc.

"We are reverting back 50 years here, my friends, to village days. Only a few of us in Cane Garden Bay are old enough to remember this island before there were cars, when news traveled only as fast as your donkey could carry you from village to village. This is what we are dealing with, folks."

Cane Garden Bay isn't what it was 50 years ago. Maybe it was self-sustaining then, but it is not now. My mind pivots back to evacuation, more resolutely now that I do not hear any mention of plans to meet the village's most basic necessities. As much as I love Cane Garden Bay and would eagerly offer my blood, sweat and tears, this plan does not seem feasible. This is not an African village, accustomed to "living off the land" with no power and no plumbing. This is a modern, affluent island with one of the highest GDP per capita in the Caribbean. It is the sailing capital of the world, where millionaires vacation on their mega-yachts and socialites toast champagne at black-tie soirées. Not to say everyone does not get along—there is little classicism that I have seen, but to assume that the entire island of 25,000 people can suddenly revert to "simple island life" and non-dependency on modern infrastructure and conveniences, or store-bought food, or flushable toilets, or the outside world, is delusional and quite frankly, impossible.

"Our first priority," the man continues, "is to prepare for Jose, which is due to hit sometime in the next few days." Now he's talking. "We have not been able to ascertain exactly when it's coming, so it's best to prepare quickly and be ready for the worst. A few community members have already required medical care due to injuries from clearing debris. Please protect yourselves in your cleanup efforts. Do NOT touch any electric lines. Some of them, as people have learned the hard way, are picking up electricity from generators and are LIVE. Remove as much debris from your property and surrounding areas as possible. Burn everything. Board up your windows and doors. As almost all our homes have been left hanging by a thread, we are all now more vulnerable to a second impact. If you have no place safe to stay, please come see me, and we will find you shelter." I wonder where . . . there are not enough bathtubs on this island for all of us to huddle into.

Slowly people begin to disband. We see Clem standing not far from the congregation, and I approach him with the bag of chips and water. "Oh, but I have food, thank you! A kind American woman cooked me a meal, and brought me water, but thank you. Thank you!" He still graciously accepts our gifts, which only affirms that he needs them.

On our walk back, Adam and I drag a few large rectangular slats of wood from the many strewn about the rubble on the road, set some aside to return for later with the car, and carry what we can on our heads back up the hill to our home. When we get in Zorro to return, Adam comments nonchalantly, "Diandra, do you notice anything different?"

It takes me a moment to look around before I realize our windshield is gone.

"Oh my God." We both start laughing. "Where the hell is the windshield?" We climb out of the car and scan the perimeter, even look down the hillside, but see no shattered glass, no glass at all.

"Irma needed a new contact lens!" I crack a joke, a welcomed diversion from our constant unease. We laugh our way down the hill, and make a successful trip hauling several more sheets of plywood on the roof of our car, one hand out the window clinging to each side. We charge the phone from the car's USB port on this short trip, greedy for every bit of battery boost we can drain, and flip through radio stations eager to find a news update on Jose. Reggaeton, Salsa music and Spanish commentary offer no consolation or information. I chuckle to myself. The irony. For a dancer who normally relishes a good jam on her daily commute, I have never been less thrilled to hear Reggaeton.

Back home, I enter our neighbor Leah's apartment for the first time. Her front and side French doors are also blown out, her floors flooded, and the roof above her kitchen and bathroom imploded, with debris hanging from the rafters. I vow to return as soon as I can to sweep, but for now I scan the room for what may be of immediate use to Adam and me, as we prepare our home. I grab a short ladder and bring it to Adam who has already begun rounding up some of the fugitive French doors from our surrounding areas, and unscrewing our neighbor's doors that are salvageable to try to jam and secure into our door frames.

Looking at the height of the frames, I gauge we will need a taller ladder. I scavenge our upstairs neighbor's home and find a tall ladder and a Swiss army knife that may be useful. On a lopsided tipped wooden shelf, I also spy several warm unscathed bottles of warm Presidente (Dominican) beer that happens to be my favorite. (Adam and I drank the remainder of our own warm beers the night before to numb ourselves to sleep.) I may be back for these, I plot deviously. I hope they will not miss them. Surely, only Adam and I are savage enough to savor warm beers. Their trash is our treasure!

Adam has managed to miraculously shove the doors, now swollen with rainwater and humidity, into the frames, which were twisted beyond repair by Irma's force. I help hold the heavy splintered sheets of wood across the doors as he drives nails through them into adjacent wooden beams. Had I known it was this easy, I would have insisted we had done this before Irma struck. It takes several hours to board up every door and window. I snap a few photos to share with my family, still more concerned with their panic levels than our own.

It is now late afternoon, and we determine that there is enough time left in the day before nightfall to drive towards town to see if we can snag a signal. Unsure of what we will find along the way, we carry a bottle of water, charge the phone and flip obsessively through radio stations to pick up a weather update. There are no USVI or BVI stations playing. We assume their radio stations were flattened like everything else. The blaring Salsa music we manage to pick up suggests that Puerto Rico may not have been hit, or at least not as badly as neighboring islands.

On the way, we pass several other cars without windshields, some crushed and roofless, far more wounded than our lucky little Zorro. Drivers stick their hands through the empty space above their dashboards and wave.

"Hey! You got a nice car, just like mine!" we all joke and laugh.

The road towards town is passable but barely so. Battered cars weave around one another and fallen electric poles, trees and scraps of fences and homes. We drive until Adam picks up a signal halfway down Joe's hill. We pull off to the side, where we see other cars have done the same. In the few minutes it takes us to climb out of the car, a slew of ten or more long text messages buzz my phone.

As I spend a few minutes scrolling through them, Adam lights up a cigarette and stares down at the decimated valley below us that now looks scorched and dead. It's difficult to judge the damage of Road Town from here, but the amount of debris speckling the hillside is not promising. All of that must have come from somewhere.

Some of the messages coming in are encouraging…

"Thinking of you… you guys are tough MFers. The BVI airport will open tomorrow at 10am. Jose veering north of you." I sigh with relief.

But as more messages roll in, they become disheartening. The ports and airports all around us have been damaged, and there are no flights until Sunday at the earliest. Jose is now a category-4 and will be passing over us Saturday between 8am and 8pm. That's tomorrow.

I tell Adam the news and we pause to think. He carefully advises me what to say. Our time, battery-life, and credit (phone minutes) are limited. Succinctness is crucial.

I message David: "Here now. Can you look into private and public options for planes, boats? Check BVI Abroad Facebook page and the BVI Community Board. No more reception at home so we made it into town. Please EVERYONE keep sending us updates and texting. My credit is limited. Trying to fortify our home but roof may go then whole place will be sucked away. Looting and violence are real possibility here. Need to leave ASAP. THINGS MAY BE WORSE AFTER JOSE."

Suddenly another batch of messages arrive, reporting that Jose is only a category-3 and may miss us entirely. It's difficult to tell when the messages were sent, which are most recent and thus accurate.

Another message reports that the British Navy is sending two ships with aid, but Darren doesn't know when or where. They are trying to find us flights, but because Irma is hammering her way north, airports in Florida are shutting down. He asks us if we could even reach the BVI airport. Good question.

I text him back: "Please send me time and date of messages as we're getting them all at once. Please EVERYBODY keep trying to call and message us to keep us updated. Just messaged David more info . . . Love you!"

Adam and I debate whether or not to drive all the way into town, and decide against it. Back in Cane Garden Bay, we pick up more giant slats of wood from the debris, and return home, where our apartment floor is again flooded. Adam notices that water from the upstairs apartment is leaking through our ceiling, which brings us to a startling realization. Our ceiling is wood, not concrete like we had thought. Furthermore, it is sodden and heavy with flood water. If any more debris from the roof above it collapses, our ceiling will most likely crush us.

Adam speaks with our next door neighbor who says his ceiling is leaking as well. This is bad. Particularly if Jose hits us as a category-4. A soggy, sinking wooden ceiling, with no exterior support, is not going to hold against a category-4 hurricane. And Irma was a category-2 two days before she struck us as a category-5. No one could possibly persuade us that Jose may not do the same.

I spend the next couple hours sweeping our upstairs neighbors' and Leah's floors, trying to lessen some of the weight from above our heads. The water in their homes is above my ankles, and it is no easy task to sweep the water from one end of their apartments all the way off the balcony on the opposite end, with a broom. Adam continues to reinforce our doors and windows, and hauls the remaining chunks of large debris from our property and burns it. Once finished sweeping, I help him as quickly as I can. There is so much stuff to clear, and so little time. The piles of books we had left laying out to dry we decide now to burn. As I cringe at the thought of chucking them, I cringe more at the thought of their decapitating us in category-4 wind speeds of 130-156 mph, according to the Saffir-Simpson scale, which we now know by memory.

"Diandra!" I hear Adam shout. "Come here!"

I run to his side where he stands on the balcony.

"Look what I see," he says, pointing across the road, 100 meters away.

Now that the leaves have all withered and died, we can more clearly see into the fallow landscape, where my guitar reflects a ray of sun, a flare gun for its own rescue. I rush to dig it out from the fallen branches, impelled by a dimming hope that it may still be playable. When I pick it up, her neck hangs limply from my hand, wrangled and broken by Irma. Adam and I take pictures of ourselves pretending to play, one last homage to an instrument that has filled our home with music, and joined countless friends and students of mine in song. Adam takes my guitar to the fire and dumps her into the flames.

The night covers Irma's gruesome crime scene like a bodybag. Adam grills the last of our meat and heats a can of beans on our stove, which we share. We crumble with exhaustion onto the chairs of our balcony and gape at the star sequined sky and the hills of Cane Garden Bay, now dotted with contained refuse fires. This small sense of satisfaction that we have done all we can to prepare for Jose temporarily abates our worry.

"Now what…?" Adam asks. I grab the flashlight and disappear upstairs to grab two bottles of our neighbor's Presidente. The warm beer tastes like champagne as it funnels down our quenched throats. We did well only to drink a half gallon of water today, despite the heat and labour we demanded from our bodies. Even so, I felt like we had splurged. Tomorrow we will drink less.

Suddenly, we spot headlights from afar, of several cars snaking stealthily through the dark, down Soldier hill into Cane Garden Bay. We wonder why anybody would be out on the road at this time, particularly if there's a curfew? I do not speak of the workings of my imagination at this time, envisioning reckless emboldened criminals, driven by desperation and rare opportunity, roving into Cane Garden Bay to pillage shops and homes.

Adam calls an end to our evening outdoors, "I think it's time for bed." When we close our only remaining openable door (the side entrance) to retire to bed, our apartment pitches into darkness, every window blinded from the light of the moon by laths of plywood. The eerie yellow glow of our flashlight as it flickers about our wretched, boarded up home reveals a scene out of a zombie apocalypse movie.

CHAPTER 8: THREE DAYS AFTER IRMA

It is Saturday, September 9th. We wake again with the sun. I make us each another egg sandwich, one egg between two pieces of bread, and coffee. We expect Jose today. We anticipate the worst, that he will be a category-4 and will destroy what is left of the upstairs apartments, now that their roof is breached. He will most likely take our ceiling as well, although whether it will be hurled away or collapsed onto our heads is yet to be determined. I run up to Leah's place and empty her cupboards of any remaining nonperishable food. If I have time, I will return and try my best to hurricane-proof her home as well, which will not be easy since all the doors are gone and it is essentially a wind-tunnel. For now, we need more information. We may even need a safer place to stay.

Before 7 a.m. we drive back down the hill and park the car. The mood has changed. The air reeks of decay, and while the excavator continues to scrape rubble from the road, the endless wreckage along the beachfront and the hillside seems to have multiplied. The last of the fallen foliage is dead and withered, baked by the sun and decomposed into a dusty desert brown. There is nothing left to hide the tattered remnants of this island.

The listless wandering of residents, the dwindling resources, and dead-end conversations rotten with rumors are draining the goodwill from this community and us. No one can yet confirm exactly when Jose is hitting nor how hard, or when aid is coming. We hear there were five deaths reported island-wide, and many people are still missing.

We pass a few friends exchanging information on the roadside in front of what they have converted from two adjacent apartments into a communal bunker. They tell us that they have heard Jose will not be coming until Sunday (tomorrow).

The conversation is rife with bitterness and agitation. Everyone feels neglected, by community leaders, by the BVI government, by the world. Where is the help? Where is the aid? Where is the information? I am amazed that not even one government representative in a truck with a bullhorn (besides Mr. Turnbull), or the police, or the firemen, or ANY agency with the responsibility of civilians' welfare has passed through Cane Garden Bay with updates. The roads are clear, and many vehicles are still intact. Why have they left everyone bereft, speculating and anxious? Surely, this will not lead to anything good. If Adam and I are feeling uneasy, and have already technically "looted" our upstairs neighbors' homes, surely others must be growing desperate, maybe even rash.

We invite whomever can fit in our car to venture to town and catch a signal. Three friends hop in and we creep up and around the hills, rubbernecking at the ramshackle homes and cars. There is too much to take in, each dissected house, uniquely carved by Irma's manic hands, a story for the evening news or a study for a scientific journal.

I feel sudden unbearable thirst and realize Adam and I left our water bottle at home. I see one friend is carrying water and ask her for a swig. "Of course!" She eagerly shares. "Take all you want. We have plenty at home!" I only take a sip, but it feels like a chug, so intensely satisfying and equally guilt-inducing. I thank her too much.

As we descend Joe's hill someone shouts, "I've got one!" and we stop the car halfway down the hill to sap the signal. Twenty more text messages from my brothers jostle my phone, a depressing deluge of logistical roadblocks.

Flights out of BVI are still halted.

Airport is closed.

No ferries or airports are operational.

Our details were shared with the U.S. Embassy, but there are no publicized evacuations.

Jose is on track to hit us this afternoon as a category-3.

There are reports of evac boats taking folks to Puerto Rico, but nothing concrete.

On a more positive note, they say they have booked us a flight on Cape Air and United Airlines from Tortola to Raleigh for Tuesday. That was the earliest option. Tuesday seems like a long way away. [We do not learn until later that they have been working 24/7 trying to book us flights, only to learn that the flights were canceled, or that the flights never existed in the first place, all the planes and airports now defunct.]

Also, posts on Facebook report that British planes and boats carrying aid workers and relief supplies have arrived, so we should keep an eye open. Where are they?

David asks how they may be able to add credit to our phones. Thankfully, our friend and journalist Katie King from the local newspaper the BVI Beacon, has already had the foresight to add a little credit to our phone (and several others'—we learn later) from off-island. David advises us to have our things packed and ready to fly out, find a safe place (a shelter, hotel or house) to wait, and stay inside and safe until we can safely leave the island. How will we know of any sudden changes or updates if we are inside hiding, devoid of communication?

We know they are trying their best from afar.

Darren writes finally, "How are things there? We are all concerned of course."

I respond, "We will be staying in Cane Garden Bay. It is now Saturday, 11:15 a.m. Thanks for the flight info. Love you." There is no need to say anything more and no reason to call, but many reasons to hurry home. Our passage off island is now arranged, and all we can do is wait.

We offer our friends without cellular service our phone to contact their families. One of them simply dictates a brief message, which I text to his family. Our friend who shared her water bottle asks to use the phone herself, we assume to send a text. We are surprised when she steps away from the car and we hear her speaking to her mother, in England. I mentally calculate how much credit that call must be sucking from our reserve, but keep quiet, trying to empathize with her poor anxious mother abroad.

Several minutes pass and they are still chatting. Adam, whom I married for his unfaltering patience, speaks up.

"Diandra, ask her to end the call. We don't have much credit."

I peek my head out the car window and call her name. She carries on. I wait a few minutes and call her name again. Still, she carries on. My patience expires.

I step out of the car and approach her, "Please, we don't have much credit. We haven't even talked to our families that long..." Come to think of it, Adam hasn't spoken to his mother at all. She spends a few more minutes "trying" to end the conversation and finally hands back the phone with forced contrition. With less forbearance, we drive home again to shut ourselves in for Jose. There is more traffic on the road now. Along the ridge between Road Town and Cane Garden Bay, we pass a friend who flags us down.

"Jose is coming tomorrow! It's a category-5!" she shouts. "Do you have someplace safe to stay?" We picture our tree-fort of a home, and unconvincingly respond, "Yes, thank you. You be safe too!" On our drive back, we warn everyone we pass of this latest update. As much as I hate to cause panic, I also cannot bear the possibility of withholding any information that could possibly protect people from further harm. Still others tell us they have heard Jose is coming in the middle of the night, but will only be a category-3 and is far north of us.

Just as we are about to turn up our road, a lanky light-brown skinned man with dark curly hair and a mustache jumps in front of the car.

"YOU!" He shouts. I was looking for you!" He is talking to me. "Where are you going? I have something for you!" He looks familiar, but I cannot recall how I know him. He is smiling excitedly and apparently very happy to see me.

"I'm sorry, but we have things to do at home," I respond kindly.

"Please come back! I will be at Myetts!" he begs us. "Don't forget! I'm so happy I found you!" Adam and I drive away, confused, until I finally place the man's face. I think I had given him a lift one time late at night, into Cane Garden Bay from the mountaintop many months ago, but never saw him again. Could it be him?

Back in our apartment I take time to rearrange the furniture in Leah's apartment in a futile attempt to fortify it against Jose. We stack all the pillows up on the kitchen counter outside the bathroom door, prepared to hide in the shower again if need be. Adam and I share a can of beans and a can of soup. In only four days, we have grown more thin, tan and dirty, from the rationed food intake, the laborious cleanup and prep, and the lack of showering. We are wary to use our water yet for bathing. If Jose doesn't kill us, we plan to haul up ocean water for taking baths and flushing toilets. We are down to three gallons of drinkable water.

We decide to drive down the hill to find our mysterious friend. If there are any early signs of Jose, we can quickly drive or even run back. When we park outside of Myetts, for the first time I feel unsafe leaving my car on the roadside. This 1992 jalopy suddenly stands out like a rare precious commodity amidst the spoils. It will be dark soon, but we vow not to tarry long. Sure enough, our tall teetering friend appears, overjoyed to hand us a large plastic bag. When I gaze inside, I see it is full of cartons of cigarettes. He also hands us two warm beers. I laugh to myself, thinking of prison movies where inmates barter cigarettes. The beer and the smokes, like our beat-up Suzuki, are now as precious as gold.

Smiling, he says, "You don't remember me, do you!?"

Sheepishly I respond, "I think so…"

"Brother," he turns to Adam, "Is this your wife?"

"Yes," Adam responds.

"Your wife is so niiiiice! I will never forget her." He pauses, smiling. "My name is Caesar, by the way."

"I'm Adam." The two shake hands.

"No worries, man, I got a woman at home," Caesar adds, beaming cheekily from ear to ear. "I just wanted to say thank you to your wife. It's times like these when you remember people who were good to you, you know what I mean?" It's standard for Caribbean men in conversation to address the husband, more than the wife, even if they know the wife better. It's a sign of respect.

Adam and I smile and nod, grateful for his praise, his company, and his gifts.

"Man, when I first moved here—I came here for work, I'm an engineer from Trinidad," he interjects, "I had no car, no friends. I was stuck in the rain at night, on the top of the hill, and I was thinking there ain't no way I'm getting a ride from NOBODY." He laughs, swigs from his own presumably warm beer, and continues speaking to Adam.

"And this little tiny white girl, all alone, not knowing me from ADAM," he pauses and nudges Adam, proud of his play on words, "stops and picks me up. I couldn't believe it!" He throws his hand to head and laughs. "I did not see THAT coming. She didn't see me as a scary black man, she just saw me as someone who needed help."

Adam smiles and nods, "That's Diandra," he says, warming my heart. After days of cinching up our home, our supplies, our purse-strings, our cell phone minutes, our hearts, this man makes me remember the impact of selflessness, and that Adam and I are generally selfless people, and should continue to be, even in hard times.

Caesar can see he's slightly embarrassing us, and concludes his story: "Anyhow, it stuck with me. And when this shit happened," he gazes at the refuse around us, "I just wanted to find her, and give her something."

"Thank you," Adam and I both say, deeply touched by his sentimentality.

"There's more warm beer over here!" Caesar, changing the subject, nods for us to follow him to a small rectangular metal cooler in the middle of the parking lot. It looks as though it was ejected like a pilot's seat before a crash, straight up and out of Myett's bar. It's dented, contorted, and cracked open, with twenty or thirty warm beers lying amidst sand and broken glass.

"Happy birthday!" Caesar sings and laughs. Adam and I dig in for two more and we all saunter towards the sand.

"Brother, things are not good. I'm worried about this place. They better get help in here, and it better come FAST. Things turn ugly in a situation like this. And I'm not talking about crime."

We listen intently.

"Look at all this waste and dirty sewage water. This is a recipe for disease. People are gonna start to get sick. I'm talking typhoid… cholera. And all this sitting water is mosquito heaven." [Mosquitos breed in sitting water. The island has had a slew of mosquito-born viruses that temporarily cripple people. Dengue, or bone-crusher as it is commonly known, had been around for ages, but more recent to enter the arena are two bigger contenders: Zika, which can cause birth defects, and Chikungunya, which mimics extreme rheumatoid arthritis throughout the entire body. Adam and I had experienced both, mine more severe, and certainly did not wish that ailment on ourselves, or anybody, for that matter.]

Just as we reach the beach, Caesar tells us he has to stop at his house but he will return. He asks if we will keep an eye on his bag, which he leaves behind. We agree and tell him we'll wait for him on the beach.

When we reach the beach, we find a few other familiar faces, including Clem, another friend, his teenage son and his friend, and a Dominican chef whom I also know from giving him the occasional lift into and out of town. We all liven up to see each other. The teenagers disappear into Myetts and return with a few bottles of top-shelf champagne they've managed to excavate from the crumbled ruins of Myett's bar. Their behavior does not seem delinquent. Having given these kids lifts to school on many days, I know them to be respectful and law-abiding. In all my work as an educator on this island, I have been constantly impressed by the remarkably good nature of Tortola's youth.

The father of the teenage boy expresses his

disappointment with the looting, but pops a bottle open nonetheless and passes us another. "In desperate times," he cheers and we all take turns swigging and passing the bottles, enjoying a few nostalgic moments of normalcy, like it's just another lazy Saturday afternoon of relaxation on Cane Garden Bay beach.

Clem laughs as he gulps down the warm champagne.

"Man oh man, what a nightmare she was," he rants mid-chug, as though remembering a violent brawl with a crazy ex-girlfriend. "200 mph winds I heard! Can you believe it? That's the speed of NASCAR!"

The father speaks more soberly, "My house is gone. I want to get my son off island to continue school—there will be no school in session here for months, but now how am I going to afford that? At least I have insurance, but who knows how long that's gonna take . . ." His speech peeters out. "What am I driveling about?" He snaps out of it. "We are ALIVE! God is good."

We all offer a cheers again. Clem thanks us again for the phone usage and the water. We truly feel lucky to have been in a position to help. There may be days soon coming when we will have to start relying on others. I do hope aid is on its way.

The Dominican chef asks if I can send a text message to his girlfriend back in Dominica that he is okay. I take her number and promise to do so once we get reception again.

As the night sets, Adam and I say goodbye and start to drive back home, unsure of whether we are more afraid of night prowlers or Jose. We stop outside of Caesar's apartment block, and Adam wanders around calling for him, carrying his bag. He returns to tell me he found Caesar, in his first floor apartment with the door wide open and candles lit, fully dressed and passed out on his bed. Maybe Caesar was a little more drunk, or distraught, than we had realized. I envy his alcohol-induced slumber and hope I can manage to fall asleep so easily.

We pass Ron Cline, the brother of our landlady and the owner of Paradise Club, and another neighbor on our drive up the hill, who both offer their homes as shelter for the night. Ron tells us he has an extra bedroom where we are welcome to stay if we feel unsafe in our home. Adam and I decline with masked uncertainty, thinking we can always make a run for it if the winds seem to be getting dangerous. We have already seen that his roof too is impaired and probably not much more secure than our own. So we cloister ourselves in for the night, and brace ourselves for Jose, ready at any moment to leap into the shower—our emergency cushions on hand for our hurricane padding.

CHAPTER 9: FOUR DAYS AFTER IRMA

What a gift to feel safe, and what a tragedy that many live their lives in constant fear of peril. In the past several months since Irma, my sensitivity to calamity and suffering has heightened to a level that, while uncomfortable, is perhaps where all of humanity's should permanently reside. It has been difficult to gauge if truly the world is falling apart, or if my heart has cracked open wider to absorb the horror that always existed.

The day after Irma struck the British Virgin Islands, Mexico buckled under their strongest earthquake of a century and two weeks later, fell to its knees as another earthquake of 7.1-magnitude killed over 200 people.

Barely two weeks after that, October 1st, 2017, a madman opened fire at a country music concert in Las Vegas, slaughtering 58 people and injuring 851.

Yesterday afternoon, in broad daylight, as I was outside walking the dog in the D.C. neighborhood where Adam and I are currently staying, a drive-by shooting left a three-year-old girl with a stray bullet in her abdomen. Irma was a car full of venomous young men with semi-automatic weapons imposing their revenge on innocent bystanders.

Disaster and human suffering abound. The media and public consciousness and the average human's working memory cannot possibly be expected to keep up, nor can or should the psyche be drowned in constant crippling empathy.

But neither should our heads and hands float naively in outer space. They are designed to solve, to help, to hold, to nurture, to share, to protect—not just one another, but this world we inhabit.

When Adam and I married, we vowed to be each others' protectors for life. We melded our lives and our worlds together to share one life, one world. Almost exactly three months after we said, "I do," we found these vows put to the test, as we sheltered one another in our shower, our lives in jeopardy, our world collapsing around us.

And yet Irma's lashing only lasted eight hours. The days of desperation that followed, while they felt like decades, were still only days. The ensuing months of post-traumatic stress and displacement were still only months.

What a gift to feel safe, your life a long book of relative ease and good fortune, wherein one small chapter includes a little peril, and merits the writing of a book, a worthy read for others with long-book lives of relative ease and good fortune.

I will describe what it is like to try to sleep soundly in a home already disemboweled by the strongest Atlantic hurricane in recorded history, waiting for her brother Jose to finish where she had left off. It cannot be called sleep. The slightest sound stiffens your body and electrifies your heart, every breeze a taunting bully backing your brain into a dark corner to tremble and cower for the next blow. Yet people sleep like this every night—those who live in war zones, or gang-infested neighborhoods, or homes haunted by domestic violence.

Needless to say, we wake on Sunday, September 10th, with joy and surprise and gratitude to be alive. I laugh ludicrously with disbelief that Jose passed too far north of us to be felt, that lives were spared, that the bony remains of this once fat and fertile island were given a chance to stay standing, albeit on wobbly arthritic knees.

Adam and I rush back to our spot halfway down Joe's hill to catch a signal, passing derelict groves of severed soursop and mango trees, which Irma was able to snap away in hours after decades of nature's nurturing. We cannot detect a signal, so we decide to use our fuel to carry us all the way into Road Town, feeling more empowered now that we have a flight booked for Tuesday. When we reach the foot of the hill and can see for the first time the obliteration of Road Town, I cry on impact. The school, the government and office buildings, the banks—all of civilization's symbols of progress and order, now hollowed and crumbling. Ashamed of my tears, and determined not to reflect the direness of the situation as we drive through throngs of downtrodden homeless Road Towners, I wipe my face. Pathetically I nod and utter to each passerby, "Glad you're okay." I recognize the vehicle inspector from the Department of Motor Vehicles, a kind happy man who always astounded me in his ability to make a trip to the DMV an uncharacteristically pleasant experience. He sees the tears in my weakened smile and smiles back large, an attempt to soften my sadness. "We have life!" he proclaims and waves. I cry more, but I manage to smile more too.

We find a signal in the parking lot outside of Village Cay Marina, where cars are flattened, creased and swathed around each other like saran wrap. We stand face-to-face with what used to be Scotiabank, now a bomb-site, broken glass jutting from its window frames like jagged teeth. We recognize two guards, regular friendly employees of the bank, guarding the outside with guns. Don't they need to be with their families? What has happened to their homes? I try to call my brother but cannot reach him.

After a few minutes of waiting around, lifelessly leaning against Zorro amidst the dusty automobile burial ground, communication from the outside world slams our hopes to the ground, weighting us with dejection that mirrors the bleakness of our surroundings. First, my brother David apologizes for missing our call—he is out golfing. I swallow distaste and remind myself that just because Adam's and my life has entered a never-ending disaster zone, that doesn't mean the rest of the world is not allowed to live a normal life, meet friends for breakfast and go for a game of golf. It does register, however, how far apart we are, not just geographically, but psychologically.

David then tells us the Cape Air flight they thought they had booked for us never existed, and that Cape Air in fact is not flying out of Tortola until September 17th, which is one week away. There are apparently British troops with supplies coming or already on the ground. He also warns us of reports that the Tortola prison was destroyed and all the prisoners are out.

"Just be cautious," he imparts. This explains why we noticed a certain suspect character, whom we knew to be incarcerated, wandering Cane Garden Bay after Irma.

Adam worries that the coastline road in Cane Garden Bay at the foot of the hill leading into Road Town may be washed away from any large surge. If that happens, everyone in Cane Garden Bay will be trapped, again.

"If Jose passed north of us, we may be due for a big swell," Adam tells me. He takes the phone to text to David: "Can you check windguru BVI and look at the swell direction and size for the next week. We are worried about any swell over one or two meters with an arrow pointed down or marginally down. Thanks."

We wait for a response, but nothing comes in. We are tempted to wait a little longer and stroll into Village Cay Bar and Restaurant where we have spent many a night toasting friends, singing karaoke, dancing Soca to the regular Friday night DJ. There may be friends in there who have more information. But it will be dark soon, so we head back home. On the way, we pick up a Jamaican friend along the ridge.

"Man, what a mess." He climbs into the car brimming with the bewilderment we all feel.

"You guys hear about Lee?"

"Who is Lee?" Adam responds.

"Hurricane Lee! Hurricane Lee! I'm not playing around —I'm getting the hell off this island, one way or another. Hurricane Lee is on its way."

"And we heard prisoners are out on the loose…" Adam quietly adds. I can tell he hates to add fuel to the fire of emotions boiling us all to the point of near hysteria. He has certainly never been a sensationalist or a gossip.

"We got Irma, then Jose, then Lee. Then I hear there's a

Maria coming. Fuck no! I'm getting the fuck OFF this island," our friend rants on.

When we reach Cane Garden Bay, we climb out with three buckets to fill with ocean water for bathing and flushing. He offers to help us, even though half their contents spill on the bumpy ride up our hill. Together we all load up the car and then he goes along his way. Two friends pass by in a windowless SUV and tell us they're trying to arrange for a dinghy ride off the island. One friend, Jay, a Californian surfer, invites us to his home later in Cane Garden Bay, which he says was "built like a fortress" and unharmed by Irma. He also relays that blocking the (only) bridge to Tortola's Beef Island airport are armed military guards, who are not allowing anyone through without proof of a departing flight, with a hard copy of the ticket and a passport photo page. How in the hell are we going to be able to print our tickets, or make a copy of our passport photos? Why aren't there armed military guards here distributing food and water? And preventing people from looting and violence, rather than blocking people from leaving the island?

Once back home, Adam and I take a saltwater shower, which feels like a lavish trip to a spa, and finally flush our putrid toilet. I try to tidy up our dank, dark, dirty home, and we share a can of beans and a container of ramen noodles. Five days after Irma, we are nearing the end of our recommended one-week supply of food and water. And we were lucky enough that our stash of food and water survived the hurricane. We do not need to voice our fears to one another. If the next flights indeed do not depart Tortola for another week, we may be in trouble. The whole island will be in trouble.

Before the nightfall corners us into our home for the remainder of the evening, we drive to Jay's apartment for company and comfort. We are feeling increasingly isolated and misinformed, or altogether uninformed. Our team of two needs to start forming alliances fast.

We drive along the seaside road as far as the broken chunks of Cane Garden Bay permit. The road is void of people, the sun is setting, and once again, we shudder as we park the car and walk the rest of the way to Jay's. Suddenly a man and a woman whom I've never seen before emerge from the beachside. I see they are scavenging through the debris in Myett's parking lot and seem to be looking for something. They are not from this bay, and so I presume they have travelled here for a reason. Perhaps their home was destroyed and they have nothing. I approach them and ask if they need anything? Are they okay?

The man speaks for them both and replies, "No, thank you. We are fine." They begin to walk away, and he stops and turns back.

"Actually, do you have an extra clean toothbrush?" I cringe to realize my suspicions were true. They literally have nothing.

"I'm sorry. We don't have an extra toothbrush. But I have extra clothes? Shoes? Anything else we can offer you?"

The man seems embarrassed he asked, and shakes his head no. "Thank you, though," he smiles with sadness in his eyes.

"The Methodist Church down that way," I point, "should have supplies. Food, water, maybe toiletries. They have offered to shelter people too," I add. His wife looks hopefully in that direction, and the man thanks me again before they walk towards the church.

In the twilight of dusk we pass Columbus Variety Store where we greet our friend who sold us the water only a few days ago. He is still panning goods from the debris and storing everything, presumably, in their adjacent home, where his older brother stands upon the second floor balcony patrolling like a watchdog. He calls down to us, possibly to divert our gaze from the vulnerable merchandise. "Good evening, guys! Are you hanging in there all right?"

"Good evening! Yes, we're doing okay. Thanks! How about you guys?" I call back as enthusiastically as my edginess allows.

"Good! Good!" His cheeriness feels equally contrived, his unblinking eyes reading our own. "You guys need anything? You have enough food and water?"

"Yes, we are okay, thank you!" I respond.

"Please, take something," he coaxes flatly. I cannot help but feel that he is encouraging us to take something as a gift, so we are less inclined to steal something from them later—not that we would have. Is he forming alliances with us, in case things get worse?

"No, really, we are okay, but thank you." Adam responds.

"Nah, nah… take a bottle of wine at least. You and your honey can curl up with your candles and a nice bottle of wine tonight," he insists. "There ain't nothing else to do…"

We are set on declining but he orders his younger brother to dig us out a bottle and hand it to us.

"Thank you! That's very kind," we say. Of course, after drinking warm beer and champagne for the past five days, we are grateful, but our gratitude is muddied by the ambiguity of his intentions.

At Jay's the mood is spooky, where he and another friend languish on the floor of their candlelit porch, pass a joint, and speculate in whispers. Jay, who lives in the fully fortified hurricane-proof home of an off-island expat, tells us he was particularly worried for his seaside neighbors before Irma. He watched the swells and knowing his home was safe and secure, was tempted to go for the surf of a lifetime, but felt that would be disrespectful of others who, beyond their own volition, were not as safe. Instead he visited his neighbors and pleaded with them to take shelter with him in his Noah's Ark of a house. They refused.

"I have plenty of food, water, booze," he told them, as he tells us now, pointing to the stack of water and wine that align his wall.

Jay recounts how he then witnessed Irma flick away all the homes from around his one by one, how through the window he helplessly saw his elderly neighbor dive into her refrigerator as her pretty pink wooden walls exploded away, how he hurried all of them into his home during the eye, and watched one with desperate hungry eyes peruse his belongings and overheard a plot to return to strip the place, and the rest of the neighborhood. I cannot tell if he is paranoid from the pot, or accurate in depicting the great economic divide of our world suddenly thrust into the smoldering cauldron by eight hours of Irma. What does happen when the haves and the have-nots scurry together like drowning rats up into the last dry gutter? Are we all about to find out?

Adam shares our recently bestowed bottle of wine with the two of them out of habitual house-guest etiquette, as I sourly eye Jay's abundant wine collection that collects dust on the rack behind him. When we finish the bottle, Adam and I head home, more distressed than before. On our walk back to the car, an oncoming car slowly rolls up beside us in the darkness. We are alarmed to see they are two heavily armed, stern-faced BVI police officers wearing camouflage uniforms and bullet-proof vests.

"What are you two doing out here?" the officer in the passenger seat barks at us, his accusatory scowl mottled with shadows by the dim dome light of their SUV.

"I'm sorry, officer. We were visiting a friend. We are on our way back now." I mutter, shaken.

"Don't you know there's a curfew? It's not safe to be out here at night. Do you have someplace to stay?"

"Yes, sorry, officer. We live up the road. We didn't know." In truth, we heard there may be a curfew imposed, but were never given specifics.

They wait and watch us, like we are dangerous marauders (or easy targets), until we drive away. As we turn onto our road, Adam tells me he is going to hammer nails face up into the wooden floorboards of our outer stairs to impede intruders.

"Adam, don't do that. What if our neighbors or their child wander over in the middle of the night, in need of help or water? Or a flashlight? Don't do that." Adam heeds my advice, but from that day on, he carries a machete in the car with us wherever we roam.

CHAPTER 10: FIVE DAYS AFTER IRMA

Couples clung and swayed in sweaty synchronization to Quito's band "The Edge" in Cane Garden Bay, while servers dodged and weaved their way through the dance floor to deliver daiquiris to suburban investment bankers and their pretty, drunk daughters and housewives. It was the spring of 2014, and of Adam's and my budding relationship, when dancing on Fridays to live music amidst tourists and locals at Quito's Gazebo, marked the end of a typical work week for us. I would normally return to Cane Garden Bay in workout attire, fresh from teaching, and meet Adam at Paradise Club, where we would guzzle up cold cocktails and a postcard sunset, and then mosey down the beach to Quito's. If the band riled us up only to finish their set too early, our energy spilling over, we would dash home, change into nightwear, and cruise to Bamboushay Lounge in Road Town for a few more hours of fun. Bamboushay was the meeting point for Tortola's young and restless, and old and restless—age is no predictor of party stamina on the islands, where unlike in the States, life trumps time. On a good night, you could jam with the Premier and his wife until the sun taps you on the shoulder to go home. Clubs have no set closing time. The fête finishes when people are too tired to dance, and for Caribbean people, particularly during Carnival, that could means days.

The ocean wanted to crash the party this night. Swells

hammered against Quito's dock like a bitter uninvited guest. But I did not notice as Adam and I grooved to Quito's tender voice and lyrics, reminding us of our collective luck on this little patch of paradise . . .

> *I'm coming back to the islands*
> *I'm coming back to the sun*
> *I got my mind made up*
> *I'm making that Tortolan run*

Quito sang of a decision he made long ago to return home after many years spent abroad as a musician and songwriter. Visitors flocked annually to hear his feel-good, at times melancholy, at other times waggish tunes. I closed my eyes and spun myself on the dance floor. When I opened them, Adam was making his own Tortolan run down to the beach. I chased behind him but stopped on the sand while he raced to the dock, thrashed from all sides by lurching waves. Two silvered-haired men in their late-sixties or early-seventies, overpowered by the strength of the sea, struggled to escort their dainty wives onto their dinghy to motor back to their boat. Adam had run out to help them. Battling the bashing waves, Adam tried to hold the boat steady enough for them to board, pounded and lashed on all sides by the turbulent swell. Just then, the sky released a torrent of rain. The entire group, including Adam, scampered back to Quito's gazebo to take shelter and wait out the rain. The men, now drenched and shivering, vigorously shook Adam's hand while the women thanked him effusively and commended me on what a kind, heroic, sweetheart of a "husband" I had. This was three years before we married. When the rain grew weary, Adam led the group vigilantly back to the dock, where he was soaked by the tumultuous sea as he tried once more to help our new friends launch their boat. The water finally proved too turbulent, and they resigned themselves to find a room onshore to bunk for the night.

I watched from the safety of the shore with a small audience of stupefied spectators, women and men, none of whom (including me) quickened to help. I knew at that moment, I wanted to marry that man.

It is now Monday, September 11th, five days after Hurricane Irma felled the British Virgin Islands, and exactly sixteen years after the twin towers and the American psyche fell to their knees. World history does not cross our minds as we stir from sleep, inhale a meager breakfast (we have decreased our portions each day as our stash grows smaller, and the days stretch on), and share the last drops from one of our two remaining gallons of warm water. Scanning the hillside from our balcony, we find our landlady's brother, Ron Cline, on the road below, his generator on the back of his truck. He has been tirelessly making trips up and down the hill each day, from his home and the homes of his neighbors to Hodge's Fuel Station in Cane Garden Bay. Although the station itself and all of its structures was washed to sea, we presume a storage tank of fuel further up the hillside must have remained intact. He glances up to us, "Don't worry. I'm getting to you guys. I'm trying to ration out power to all the neighbors, a few hours at a time."

"Thank you, but we really don't need it. You can give power to somebody else who may need it more. But thank you!" We truthfully don't need it. We are surviving without lights, and we have no food remaining to keep cool in the fridge. Meanwhile, we still have ocean water to flush the toilet and bathe.

Soon we see Leah and two other friends roll up the road in a beat-up white car.

"LEAH!!" I call down to her. They stick their hands out the windows and call up to us. I immediately grab the nonperishable foods I had scavenged from her cupboards and throw them into a bag. I meet Leah in the driveway, where we hug again—it seems like ages since we have seen one another, although it's only been a few days. With tears in my eyes, I shamefully hand over her bag of food.

"I'm sorry, Leah. I stole this from your cupboards. I was worried Jose would destroy your place so I tried to salvage any food I could." She also wipes away tears and laughs.

"Oh honey, you can have them. Please! I'm just grabbing a few items and then I'm trying to get off island. Please, take anything from my apartment that you guys need."

Leah pulls out a bottle of hard liquor from her cabinet as she crawls around the wreckage of her apartment. She sees that I tried to hurricane-fortify her home for Jose, quite inadequately, but she still thanks me.

"Here! Pass it around!" she cries out deliriously, handing me the bottle, and grabs some belongings to throw into a bag. Adam, in turn, invites them to scour our home for anything that may be of use. Our tall Dutch friend hesitates to ask, "Actually, do you have a pair of shoes?"

"What size?" Adam calls out before disappearing and returning with a pair of sneakers.

For the next twenty minutes, we all sit together on whatever chairs we can drag out of the debris, or whatever we can use as chairs, and pass the bottle back and forth, gazing with disbelief over the shredded view. We hear more survivor stories, stories that rattle the soul. Soon, our companions leave to return to one of the few relatively untouched homes on island. Everybody is trying to get out someway or another, so when we part, we understand that we may not see each other for a long time—or, depending on how life unfolds, perhaps ever again. There are too many goodbyes to say, so we don't say any at all. When we all part, we will drift far from one another, stretched across the continents. From our hillside road alone, our neighbors will scatter back to France, Scotland, Switzerland, Australia, South Africa, St. Vincent, St. Thomas, Latvia, Serbia, Mexico, Jamaica, Canada, U.S.A. and England.

Adam and I drive into Cane Garden Bay around noon with the machete under the passenger seat and futilely try to catch a cell signal or dredge up more information from the community. We see a mob of neighbors, mostly employees or family members of the Rhymer family, attempting to clear the parking lot of Rhymer's Hotel and Restaurant. We immediately stop and begin helping. They warn us to be careful not to cut ourselves, as so many of the wooden planks are pierced with sharp nails threatening to plunge into our hands as we dig debris out from the mud.

We help for thirty minutes, thinning the endless mounds of refuse from the unrecognizable lot, which on a typical day, would have been tightly packed like Lego pieces with bright, tropically colored taxi buses shuttling flocks of tourists to the beach. I find a keychain that proudly proclaims, "Nature's Little Secret," the motto of the BVI. Unable to toss it on the heap, I offer it to a young Tortolan girl who clings to her mother's lap in what used to be the entrance to their gift shop. She smiles, peers at her mother for approval, and accepts the souvenir.

We promise to return, a promise we end up breaking, and continue on into Road Town, where we head directly to Village Cay Marina. Outside, I message my brother:

"Heard rumours documentation is needed to pass airport guards. Can you send some kind of confirmation with our names on it? [When they can actually book us a flight.] Confirmation code too? Also heard a rumour that only Liat is flying out. Can you call Cape Air to confirm they're flying out of Tortola?"

Inside, there are ten or fifteen regulars ambitiously sweeping up the last traces of Irma's drunken rampage through the bar. They constitute a mixture of boat owners and crewmen, sailors, and charter captains, who have lost their vessels, their livelihoods, and for some . . . their lifelong investments. Driven by community zeal and empowerment over an otherwise powerless predicament, they tirelessly haul one sloppy load of muck after another with buckets or their bare hands to the over-towering dumpster in the parking lot. Soca pumps from the miraculously intact, fully stocked bar (maybe the only one on island), while the impeccably dressed manager of the restaurant supervises, dangling the carrot of inebriation, and a sense of normalcy, before their dry throats and broken spirits.

"One free drink for workers! Keep it going!" she encourages coolly from the perimeter. Over her shoulder she quietly orders the bartender, "Don't serve a drink until this place is clean."

We see our friend Clem, the tourist from Philadelphia, his back slumped against the wall, his face clouded with concern.

"Clem! What's wrong?"

"Oh, oh. What a mess. It's just . . . not good ..." his voice seems to crumble with his body. "So I came early this morning and boarded the ferry to St. Thomas. But when we reached St. Thomas, we were turned around. I don't understand . . . I'm an American citizen. I have my passport. And there were many other Americans on board. How can they turn Americans away from American soil? I argued and kept begging to please let me enter. 'I'm an American! Here is my passport! I'm an American!' But nobody cared. They turned us all away."

I step aside to message my brother the news. Surely, this is illegal. I ask him to post and share. St. Thomas is a U.S. territory and cannot deny American citizens from entry—particularly if they are fleeing disaster. I cannot imagine St. Thomas can be worse, and, in fact, it is not, but we cannot confirm this until later.

"This needs to hit the news," my fingers fire, my face hot with the fury of injustice.

I begin to help clear debris when my phone erupts with messages, so I dart to the parking lot where the signal is stronger. Adam stays to help the others.

The text from David reads: "For Monday and Tuesday, all arrows point left." This is good regarding the swell. This means the road in Cane Garden Bay is at less risk of being washed away, and that we might still have access into Road Town, the ferry, and the airport.

"United confirmed. You are flight 6504 from Tortola to San Juan [Puerto Rico] at 10:05am. Cape Air Flight 1173 to Newark, and flight 1030 to Raleigh. Cape Air website says no service until 17th. We are checking on it now. Fuck. Just called Cape Air. They have no service out of Tortola until the 17th. This was your first flight tomorrow."

My stomach coils as though punched in the gut. My eyes sting with tears.

I respond: "Can you try Liat? Please start brainstorming

another option. Thanks bro. Love you. Even private charter flights."

"It says no charters at the moment. We are looking at Liat," David responds.

Remembering that I have a good friend, Caitlin, who works in the State Department, I implore my brother to contact her for help and report that St. Thomas is denying entry to U.S. citizens.

"Also, Intercaribbean may have flights Wednesday or Thursday? Island birds as well," I add.

There is a lull in messages from my brother, who (I later learn) coordinates frantically at home with family to find flights, only to cycle endlessly through contradictory listings, illegitimate bookings, cancellations, contended refunds, and arguments with clueless agents.

I rejoin Adam to scour away the last of Irma's slovenly footprints from the Village Cay restaurant. When the job is done, everyone crowds the bar to claim that promised cold beverage. I notice the bartender charges a few of them, unable to remember who had helped and who had not. But I say nothing, nor do I cast judgment on the amount of beers crossing the bar. For everyone, slackened by the oppressive heat of a September tropical sun, a cold drink after six days without, is heaven. Even on an average Caribbean day, liquor is cheaper and more plentiful than fresh drinkable water—a valuable commodity anywhere in the world, but particularly on islands with no freshwater rivers or lakes, surrounded by saltwater. This is why the pirates and sailors of old drank rum instead of water. Having destroyed ports and shipping vessels and airports, Irma has upped the ante, and potable water is perhaps more precious to us all than ever before.

Adam and I share a free Coke and we sit with two friends on the outdoor elevated veranda overlooking the marina, now a graveyard of sailing vessels. Sailors, who have spent their lives harnessing and honoring the forces of nature, now kneel to her dominance. They inspect their mangled overturned boats, the few that haven't sunk or been swept out to sea, with sheer despair and disbelief. Belly-up like dead whales, the million-dollar catamarans bob and groan, half-submerged under the iridescent oil-streaked water. Some are cracked in half and stacked like driftwood, fiberglass grinding on fiberglass, croaking with the current. Others drift like senile seniors further and further away from the shore, from hope of rescue, of repair, of reclamation. Most of their masts are missing or splintered into pieces, like the spirits of their owners. A grief-stricken charter captain claws himself aboard upon the hull of his catamaran called Bliss, now completely upside down, and balances on its rocking corpse in his own despair. Another middle-aged white man in khakis and a cotton tee crouches on the sidewalk below us, his head in his hands. He is whimpering aloud, "I just can't believe this. I just can't."

All we can speak of is the chaos, the uncertainty, the daunting logistics of how this island is ever going to recover, how we are all going to get out of here. A Greek sailor and gregarious friend of ours, named Achilles, around the age of fifty, approaches us with a ludicrous smile stretched across his face, which has been wrinkled by sun and laughter, his brown eyes lit with an interminable youthfulness.

Crossing his muscular weathered forearms across his waist, he gazes out, awestruck. "This is a record-breaker, my friends. This was not a category-5. This was a category-7. I have never seen this. No one has."

For a man who has sailed the world for several decades, his word carries serious weight, even amongst the most seasoned sailors. He adds, "Well, no one's coming to fetch me. I'm Greek! Ha ha!" We laugh at the thought of the Greek government organizing an evacuation, but I secretly wonder how he will fare.

I'm wearing a bright green t-shirt that says, "TORTOLA LOVE," trying, as always, to bring a little brightness to my surroundings, particularly now that my surroundings are so grim. Brighten up your corner, as they say in Ghana. A Tortolan friend who is a doctor passes by.

"Ha!" He heckles, seeing my shirt. "You still love Tortola?"

The answer leaps from my mouth in an instant. "Heck yeah. Even more now. Tortolans are strong! To survive

Irma? Amazing." He smiles with surprise and raises his bottle to mine.

"Glad to hear it," he says, "Cheers."

Osprey aircrafts circle above our heads and we begin to see armed military in camouflage march along the boardwalk below us. We sparingly take turns buying one another beers, all of us on near-empty stomachs (and wallets), so we do not need much to enjoy its effect. I distractedly try to listen to each person's plight, glancing anxiously at my phone for incoming messages from my family of encouraging news.

"The First Bank ATM is working!" someone from the crowd announces. We decide to take out more cash before we head back, unsure of what there is to actually buy on island. But certainly, it is good to have more cash on hand. Someone else tells us that he heard one petrol station on the way to the airport has fuel.

After sitting around for three hours, I have to pee, urgently. I walk to the restaurant's bathroom only to find it's closed. So I approach the bar and ask the bartender, "Excuse me. The bathrooms are closed. Where should I go?"

The woman looks at me as though I asked a stupid question. "Hold it, honey."

"Excuse me? That's not possible."

"Sure it is," she coldly responds, "I've been holding mine all day."

Having lived in "third world" conditions in Ghana for three years, in a village that had no flushing toilets or running water, the problem of a sizable population having nowhere to go to the bathroom seems like an important and easy one to solve. There are toilets here, which is more than what many developing countries have. There are buckets and ocean water to manually flush. Thanks to Irma, Tortola has suddenly regressed to developing world status, yet people do not seem prepared to face this reality. Nothing good will come of 25,000 people urinating and defecating anywhere they like. I find it remarkable that six days into Irma's aftermath, a place of business serving countless drinks has not considered this.

I respond to the woman. "Well it's not healthy to hold

your urine, nor is it possible." I curtail my tongue from adding, Surely you can't be serving drinks all day to all these people who just cleaned up your bar and are spending money, and have no place for them to pee? You can figure out how to keep beers cold and make money, but not how to keep your toilets operational?

"You can hold it," she repeats herself cuttingly, while she waits on another customer.

"Listen," I lean into the bar and look her in the face. "I asked you out of RESPECT, since I don't want to DISrespect your establishment. Where do YOU recommend I take a piss? I can pull down my pants right here if you like, but I'm sure you have a better place in mind."

The men at the bar, who have been listening intently, interject with alarm, "Noooo!! Don't do that!" The woman walks away as Adam calmly rescues me from an altercation.

"Let's walk down the boardwalk—we'll find someplace," he calmly suggests, his hand on my back.

We walk along the water until we find a grassy area where I can lower my pants and relieve myself. This boardwalk, normally a pathway taken by suit-clad businessmen and women returning from lunch to their office jobs, now a makeshift open-air public toilet. I squat with disdain, peer around to ensure my "privacy," and grumble quietly, *Even the poorest villages in Africa have more dignity than this.*

When we return, a string of dismal messages illuminates my phone.

"United, Cape Air, and Liat have no flights to San Juan tomorrow. We may be able to get you there Wednesday, though you will miss your United flight to Newark. United says that Cape Air is running, but Cape Air told me 'no.' I sent Island Birds information and a quote request in case they can get you to San Juan by 1:45 p.m. tomorrow afternoon. Waiting to hear back. I also texted Caitlin to see if she knows of any way to get you to San Juan for that flight tomorrow."

I read aloud the messages to Adam, who stares back, his face glazed with sudden austerity.

"Diandra, I know your family is trying, but they need to take further action. I will message my mom too, although I wanted to leave her out of this—too much worrying. PLEASE, tell them we need to get out of here. Tell them to CALL Caitlin. They have to work hard on this, even if they have to take a few days off of work, or quit their jobs . . . I don't think they get the severity of the situation."

More British military scuffle by sporting semi-automatic rifles, combat boots, camouflage fatigues and berets. I jump from my seat and run down to speak with a soldier.

"Please, sir! Thank you for being here!" One brawny Bajan man steps aside from the procession and listens to me. "We are Americans, trying to get to San Juan tomorrow and haven't heard any news of evacuations or ferries leaving. Do you have any information?"

His soldier's face softens as he looks at me. "Head to the airport first thing tomorrow morning, Ma'am. That's all I can say. Good luck."

"Thank you," I call to him, as he has already marched on to whatever presumably more pressing task looms ahead.

The sun will set soon and we need to get home, where we will lose communication until tomorrow. I think of what I can say to my family, to try to paint a picture of our desperation.

"Leaving Road Town in ½ hour. Fuel in car, food, water low. CALL Caitlin. I know everyone is working but please this needs to be a priority. Your jobs will understand. Any way we can get to San Juan for that flight tomorrow. We'll check messages as early tomorrow morning as we can (there's a curfew in force 6pm-9am), and then just head to the airport. If Caitlin can get our name on a list for evacuation. Adam's mom is trying too. Please communicate with her. 600+ people trying to leave. Love you. I know you're trying…"

We offer to take Clem back with us. He insists that he wants to spend the night in Village Cay on the floor in order to be in town early the next morning for a better chance of evacuation. Worried for his safety, we are finally able to convince him to come with us when we promise to bring him back first thing 7:00 a.m. the following day. Back in Cane Garden Bay, after we have dropped off Clem, Adam and I are about to turn up the road to our home when Adam says, "Stop the car."

He peers with fierce concentration towards the beach, where my eyes follow. I pull over and we step out. As we tread cautiously towards the beach, we see a small reconnaissance boat, similar to a Zodiac used by Navy Seals, approach the shore under the emerging moonlight. Four people—they look like soldiers—jump out and drag the RIB onto the sand. We watch as they cross the beach diagonally and head for the roadside. As they near us, we can see they are indeed soldiers, dressed in camouflage. I want to speak to them, but Adam tells me to hold back. They are walking quickly in the opposite direction so I sprint to catch up. As I run behind them, in the dark, I realize how stupid this is. What is to stop them from thinking they're being attacked? It's certainly not wise to surprise four soldiers from behind in a disaster zone. So I decide to shout and unabashedly announce my approach.

"Hello!! Excuse me! Please!!" They stop and turn around, and I see one of them is a woman, which strangely brings me such comfort, like she is a childhood friend.

"Hello!" I catch my breath.

"Yes?" they respond in British accents, their faces serious but intrigued.

"Hello! I just wanted to say…." panting, "Thank you for being here. I live here. My husband and I," I look over my shoulder to Adam, "WE live here, in Cane Garden Bay. And thank you for being here. We were beginning to feel abandoned."

"Oh, okay. You're welcome." They seem to be caught off guard, unsure what to make of me, of this foreign disaster zone where they have been dropped. "So far, it seems like you've got a nice little village here."

"Thank you," I respond, and think to myself sadly, I wish you could have seen it before. "Thank you, again, and goodnight." I let them walk away into the dark.

By the time Adam and I make it home, the sun has long

ago buried itself in the sea. We miss the chance to cook with the daylight, so Adam manages to heat our last can of beans by the torchlight of my mobile phone. Side by side, we pass the can back and forth taking turns scooping out our daily dose of nutrition and stare into darkness. Having charged my phone in the car, I set the alarm for 6:30 a.m. and rest it by my weary head. Adam scoops me closer to him and curls me up against his chest. We fall asleep to the chirping tree frogs and tell ourselves that all is well.

CHAPTER 11: SIX DAYS AFTER IRMA

It is Tuesday, September 12th, six days after Hurricane Irma eviscerated Tortola and changed our lives forever. I am surprised to see Adam make the bed as we pack up any belongings that survived Irma that we may wish to someday retrieve into three small suitcases and set them next to our closet. Normally I am the one to make the bed and tidy our home. Adam is the cook. I am the cleaner. These are the domestic roles we naturally assumed from our first days of cohabitation. There was never any discussion—it just happened that way. Life as a couple has always fallen into place easily for us until now. When he is not looking, I watch him delicately stretch the sheets up to the headboard, his broad muscular back built for much heavier tasks. I gaze around our broken home and back to him and am suddenly weakened with gratitude and a strange sense of nostalgia for our quaint little home and quaint little life. I fight back tears and resume preparing our "evacuation bag."

Any clothes or linens or possibly useful belongings that can be used by the community, we throw into a garbage bag to deliver to the Methodist Church on our way into town. Adam hides a few cans of food under the bed in case we are not able to make it off island and need to return that day or in days to come. There is a real possibility our home could be scavenged in our absence and the last of our food taken.

We carry a pillow, our last gallon of water, a plastic Ziploc bag with our phone, toothbrush, credit cards and cash into the car. We haven't heard any updates of the east end of the island where the airport is, so we hope for the best, but prepare for many possible scenarios. (Irma has made us very good at this). We may be prevented from reaching the airport due to blocked roads, insufficient documentation, or worst-case scenario, looting or rioting. We may reach the airport but not be able to fly out today, or for many days. Although we have heard there is a gas station open on the east end, this could prove to be untrue—as so many of the rumors over the past six days have been—in which case we will probably not use our fuel to return home, a 45-minute drive away, but instead sleep in our car at the airport until we can get out.

After the car is packed we check our home one last time to see if there is anything else to be done, anything else left to stash or stow away, any more possessions we may try to shove into our already busting tote bags. We heard evacuation planes normally only allow one small carry-on. Our bags are too big, we know, and we are prepared to have to take things out and leave them behind in the airport or in the car if necessary. Anything we leave in the car will most likely be taken, as our windshield is an open invitation for exploration. If we do leave the island, we certainly hope someone will help themselves to our remaining food, water, hell, they can take the car. Zorro has served us well and may possibly make life easier for the next family.

In the difficult process of deciding what to take with us and what to leave behind, we have prioritized our possessions according to security, sustenance, and finally, sentimentality. I carefully select photographs of my grandfather, a World War II veteran who fought in the Battle of the Bulge, recently departed at age ninety-eight, and other cherished old family photographs, and slide them between my laptop, hard drive and a few articles of clothing. On our way out the door, I feel the urge to leave behind a note. In fact, I want to write a letter to the entire island, telling them how sad we are to leave, how sick with guilt we feel, how much we do not want to leave, but how we feel we will be a burden on resources, blah blah blah. Instead I write two separate letters: one to our neighbor detailing where we have hidden food and welcoming them to anything in our home, and one to our landlady and her brother, thanking them profusely for offering us electricity and explaining the "renovations" we needed to make on the home to protect us from Jose, the boards and doors we savagely hammered into the exterior of our once beautiful little villa.

Adam and I then lock the door from the inside and leave the key on the kitchen table. The bedroom window is easily opened so we know we can return if need be, and anyone can enter for any reason. We drive down into Cane Garden Bay and stop outside Clem's hotel, but a neighbor tells us he hitched a ride into town early, so we carry on.

Soon we reach the wasteland of Village Cay's parking lot where we await incoming messages to determine our next move. Adam disappears into the restaurant to see if he can find Clem. As soon as Adam is out of sight, leaving me alone, a thin disheveled man I do not recognize who has been leaning despondently on a flipped car suddenly begins trudging towards me through the otherwise empty lot. I have never felt unsafe here or anywhere on Tortola, but I feel unsafe now. His eyes slant towards the ground as though he pretends not to see me, meanwhile beelining straight towards me, and I know there is nothing else around that he could be approaching. I do what I have done in the past when I have found myself alone in possibly dangerous situations with suspicious strangers. I shout a ridiculously friendly greeting, bordering on lunacy. "GOOD MORNING SIR! HOW ARE YOU?!?"

He looks up, startled, and slows his pace. "Good morning. I'm cool, thanks," and he veers towards the road. I do not relay this to Adam when he returns, dismissing it as paranoia, and quite frankly, feeling ashamed. Maybe the man was going to ask for help, and I frightened him away. Maybe he needed water, or a few extra dollars, or food, or like the couple we met in Cane Garden Bay, (who would have never asked, unless we had first offered), a toothbrush? Adam and

I could quite possibly be in a situation soon where we may have to start asking for help, which makes me ponder, Why are we really leaving? Are we afraid of being hungry and thirsty? Are we afraid of physical danger? Are we afraid of fighting for resources? Or are we simply afraid of asking for help? Again, we are lucky to have never had had to ask for help before, secure in our illusion of autonomy and independence. Nothing like a natural disaster to make you realize how interdependent we all are, how interdependent our precious little planet is.

Finally my phone begins vibrating with the crucial updates we need from my brother. Like scavenging for sustenance from a bucket of slop dumped at our feet, we sift through the scrambled messages:

"Monday 7:45pm: contacted liat, intercaribbean, cape air, united, island birds [airlines]. There are no flights going in/out. Cape air said maybe resume on 18th [six days away].

Brendan is contacting his associates too [Brendan is my cousin who is the sales director of a private jet rental company], and Caitlin is searching through state dept for evac. No flight is scheduled for you this week.

Diandra!! Got a secret Facebook message from Jenn Hart. Her and Darrel are doing secretive evacs to st. croix, and will take you if u get to nanny cay well before noon and find their boat. It leaves at noon.

Tuesday 6:40am: Caitlin sent me state dept info. They are doing evacs from eis [Tortola's Beef Island airport] 7:30am - 2, expect long waits. Children elderly and med emergencies first

State dept does not say where ppl are headed

They can take you both to a hotel named Tamarind Reef. Damage is minimal, and airport is open. Jenn gave your names to security. If you have any trouble, tell security that Lisa or Miles Sutherland (GM) have your names.

She said they might be doing a trip Thursday as well. If you don't do this, you may be on Tortola until flights (may) resume next Monday the 18th.

Back up plan: I got a call from Nicky, friends with Cid Nava. They are chartering planes to Puerto Rico, 5pm tomorrow, $500 per person, and they need photo of passport. I think the free boat ride sounds better tho. Let me know what you think! I think Nicky's # is ------------. Spots may fill up quick.

*Micky

Lucy Weidner is one friend who reached out to me.

Ok they said evac is going to San Juan Puerto Rico

7:30am Summary: I would take the boat to st croix or head to eis and get State Dept evac to SJ. We can get u home from either of those soon.

Jenn has accommodations for u in croix. I don't know the details in SJ."

I read the messages aloud to Adam and our brains rapidly fire up a plan. Initially, the boat trip to St. Croix sounds the most appealing. Not only does it offer us the safety and comfort of being with dear friends (Jenn and Darrel), but it seems the most guaranteed exit from this mayhem. If evacuations from the airport began at 7:30 a.m. and are expecting masses of people, we may have already missed our chance, as it is now 7:45 a.m. and we won't reach the airport until 8:45 am at the earliest, if we are able to make it there at all. We cannot understand how anybody could reach the airport by 7:30 a.m., if there is a curfew in effect (which we have already dared to break) until 9 a.m.

I message my brother that we are leaving Road Town (and losing cellular reception) to head to the airport, and will update him if possible when we arrive.

We drive towards the East End and pass the gas station that had been reported to be open for business. This time, the rumor proves true and there are cars snaking a half-mile down the road, patiently waiting in line to hoard as much fuel as their tanks and jerry-jugs can carry. We decide to bypass the line, take our chances and continue on to the airport with what fuel we have in order to snag an evacuation flight.

The East End is surprisingly tame, although as we expected, the damage to homes more dire, as many of the dwellings in this area of the island were less solid structures than elsewhere. At the bridge connecting Tortola to Beef Island, where the airport concludes our long treacherous journey like the Emerald City, there is indeed a checkpoint where two young military guards in camouflage carrying automatic weapons block our passage. We stop, hoping they do not turn us around for breaking curfew. They politely ask to see our passports—thank God they survived Irma—and ask us what brings us there. Although it seems like an obvious answer, we tell them we are hoping to evacuate. With sincere empathy, they hand us back our passports and utter gravely, "Good luck."

At the airport, we find a vacant spot along a side road and park the car. From afar we can see a swarm of families with suitcases stretched across the entrance of the airport. We brought the Tortola Dance Project vinyl parade banner from the Emancipation Festival to cover the windowless face of our car. We lock the doors and leave the bags in the backseat.

"Let's just run in and check out the situation. If we can bring the bags, I'll run back and get them while you hold our place in line," Adam strategizes. We race to join the others who mill about with glazed faces, peering through the glass. The doors to the airport are closed, although we see people inside. Familiar faces greet one another and everybody asks the same question: "How are you getting out of here?"

Some benevolent cellular tower somewhere bestows upon us a signal. I shoot a message to David: "8:39 am Just got to airport. It's still closed but lots of people waiting outside. May stay here to see if we can get evacuation to SJU [San Juan airport, Puerto Rico] and try to catch our UA flights [that my mom had booked] all the way to Raleigh. If not may try to go to Nanny Cay and catch boat to st croix"

David relays dispiriting news: "Yo sorry, mom cancelled your 1:45 flight out of SJ, but there is another at 3 we can book if u may take it"

My emotions erupt hastily. "Wtf. This info is important. We wouldn't have wasted our fuel to make a trip out here. Okay still gonna try to get the evac to SJU."

Moments later, David writes: "3pm flight is still open tho. Get to PR!"

Finally, official-looking men and women emerge from the airport and begin posting signs with tape onto the concrete outer walls of the airport. They are careful not to let anyone inside.

"Barbados Evac"

"Jamaica Evac"

The moment the dutiful agent walks away, the humid Caribbean air debilitates the feeble scotch tape and the posters flit away. I grab them and try to repost, to no avail, so I let the breeze take them.

"Diandra Jones?" I hear an unfamiliar voice call my name. "Diandra Jones?" he repeats. A few meters away, a pudgy white man with a gentle face calls my name among others. He wedges one foot in the door and one foot out onto the concrete patch of refugees, his thick auburn hair stuck with sweat to his forehead.

"That's ME!" I shout. I race to him and he looks at me with doubt.

"*You're* Diandra Jones?"

I can only imagine, as has happened many times in my life given the African-American quality of my name, that he expected a black girl. Amongst a predominantly black crowd, I wonder if he thinks this white girl is an imposter, cutting the line for a ticket out of here.

"Yes, I'm Diandra Jones," I say, trying not to project the unfounded guilt he has imposed on me. He doesn't look convinced.

"What's your hometown, Diandra Jones?" he asks. He is wearing a collared, short-sleeved, light-blue shirt with the emblem of a private charter service. I wonder what his affiliation is? He doesn't look like a representative from the U.S. government. Maybe he works for a private charter plane company and is an associate of my cousin Brendan. Maybe he is a friend of Cid Nava and will be asking $500 per head for a flight to PR. Either way, we are ready to go with him.

"Erie, Pennsylvania," I respond. "I'm here with my husband, Adam Stauffer, also American."

He glances down at his clipboard. "Okay, Diandra. I think we're going to be able to get you out of here today. You hang tight." He steps back inside.

I return to tell Adam who bolts back to the car to fetch our bags. While I wait for his return, I spot a slender, balding white man wearing a U.S. government fluorescent vest appear from the door. I hesitate to push our luck and double-dip into rescue missions, but decide it's worth investigating. I approach him timidly, fearing reproach, assuming he must be as distressed and tired as the rest of us. Much to my surprise, he questions me with overwhelming tenderness.

"You okay, honey? You're American? Okay... you have your passports? Okay, don't go far. We're here from the U.S. government. We can get you to Puerto Rico. And don't worry, we'll have some food and water for you."

I ask him about bags—can we bring one? If so, how big? He peers down the line to Adam who has just raced back. Sweat now darkening his shirt, he waves wearily, hauling two hefty bags, one on each shoulder.

"Yes, that should be okay.... We don't have a full plane, so you guys are lucky. I'm just waiting a few more minutes to see if any other Americans show up. If not, you can bring your stuff, and we'll get off the ground."

He meanders away, bellowing through the crowd like a peanut-vendor at a ballgame, "Any Americans? Any U.S.

citizens?" There are surprisingly none. No one else had any idea that the U.S. was evacuating that day. How could they? There has been a complete breakdown of communication on island. We only knew of the evacuation because my dear childhood friend Caitlin, who was one of my bridesmaids only three months prior, works for the State Department, and my brother Darren had placed our names on a list with the U.S. Embassy. Otherwise, we too, would have remained in the dark, scraping the bottom of a can, and shaking the final drops from an empty water gallon into our dry throats.

Adam and I now wait. An American friend of ours approaches us. She is empty-handed and assessing the situation. She tells us she left her husband and son at home and just took the initiative to come to the airport to see what was going on.

"Are they allowing people to bring luggage?" she asks. I point to our bags and explain they are permitting these because the plane is not yet full. "But we have so much stuff . . . " she responds. Indecision shadows her face. Just then, the U.S. agent calls us over.

We enter the airport and see only a few other Americans filling out paperwork, commissary notes, consenting to repay the U.S. government for the cost of the flights. One of them is Clem. We are relieved and grateful that he made it on this flight—our shared journey through disaster soon to reach its end.

Once aboard the flight, a snazzy G5 jet plane, we realize the burly man with the light-blue shirt is one of many pilots who have been taking turns evacuating civilians for the past week from all the hurricane-ravaged islands. They tell us that St. Maarten was the worst they've seen, followed by Tortola, and then St. John. They also tell us how the Puerto Rico government raced to repair the damage to its airport from Irma in order to serve as a hub for evacuations for all other incoming Caribbean hurricane refugees.

One of the pilots then steps into the cabin and squats beside the passengers. Speaking softly, he explains that we will soon be taking off, and to brace ourselves. Due to the short runway, this jet will have to accelerate very quickly in order to clear the tarmac. Moments after he returns to his seat, the plane throttles and we are riveted against our seats by the force of the engine as the jet careens across the runway and lifts off.

Soon they offer us a choice of cold water or soda. I cannot help but cry. I try to wipe my face and disguise my desperation, my ridiculous joy in savoring a cold beverage, my overblown gratitude in accepting such a seemingly trivial gift, which now carries immense physical value and emotional potency. There is a remarkable thing that happens when you are full of grief, and someone extends you sympathy. It's like poking a tiny hole in a monstrous bulging water balloon. You are so taut with pain and so easy to puncture with the finest point. It is a terribly fragile feeling and at the same time, refreshingly human.

At the Luis Munoz Marin International Airport in San Juan, Puerto Rico, we and the other nine passengers disembark. I hug our pilot and ask to take a picture with him. He consents with a warm smile, finding our superfluous gratitude both alarming and endearing. Once inside, we file through a narrow hallway of relief workers to customs. Our customs agent, a thin, shaved-head, handsome Puerto Rican speedily processes us, stealing curious glances of awe and pity.

Adam asks him, "How many hurricane refugees have you been taking in?"

"About 5000 a day, mostly from St. Maarten," he sighs as he hands us back our passports, his own exhaustion pulleyed by duty and compassion.

Finally an escalator submerges us into the inner sanctuary of the San Juan Airport. At its foot in the baggage claim area stands a solo soldier in fatigues. To our left we see two long parallel lines of men and women, presumably other evacuees waiting. Adam and I wait for instruction, so grateful to be in some semblance of order and civilization, we could probably have waited for days. Suddenly, the soldier speaks: "Excuse me, what are you guys waiting for?"

"We're not sure... we just were evacuated from the British..."

He cuts us off. "Yes. You can go ahead," and directs us towards the people. We follow instructions and prepare to fall in line with the others. The next moments will forever be ingrained in the cells of our beings, and forever leave us indebted to people of Puerto Rico. Nearly one hundred people turn to face us in a human tunnel of love. "Welcome home!" they cheer. Some hold signs that echo this sentiment: "You are home. You are safe. Welcome."

I quicken my step, slightly embarrassed, again feeling like my balloon is being punctured, but this time by many many fine points from all directions. My eyes and ego cannot hold back the tears and I weep uncontrollably, wishing my hat was large enough to hide my whole face, my whole body. I cannot bear the rawness of this emotion. This compassion from so many strangers is nearly incapacitating. I turn back to see Adam. He too is wiping away tears.

In the weeks to come, when Hurricane Maria rips through Puerto Rico leaving many parts of the island in shambles—to this day, nine months later, still in shambles—we shudder with writhing pain, anger and disgust at how the U.S. government turned their backs on these generous people.

Upon passing the last cheering, smiling stranger, another stranger approaches us to offer cold beverages, food, clothing, toiletries. There are tables surrounding the perimeter of the room stacked with goods donated by the public and by the Red Cross. Another Puerto Rican man approaches us and offers us his personal cell phone to call our family, which we accept with gratitude. We contact our family and tell them we have made it to safety.

With magic and ingenuity, they manage to book us a flight to Newark and then to Raleigh, North Carolina. In the Puerto Rico terminal, we see other U.S. and British Virgin Islanders with their families, haggard and drained, slumped in vinyl airport seats, the tranquility of their surroundings granting them their first opportunity after a week of mental and physical anguish, to take a breath. For the entire duration of the flight from Puerto Rico to Newark, a twenty-something white Bostonian man from St. John brags with bravado for all to hear about Irma's power and his own MacGyver skill in engineering the survival of himself, his wife and young child. It is not until the flight lands and we are standing that we spot a friend from Tortola seated two rows behind us. She remains seated while everyone else rustles for their bags. I call her name and she turns her doleful gaze from the window to us. I get the feeling she had spotted us long ago, but chose to cloister herself with grief in her seat.

"Are you okay?" I ask, feeling the inadequacy of my inquiry.

"Yeah, I'm okay. You guys?" We nod with an enervated smile.

"I am just so mad. Furious…" she swallows back tears and her eyes seek composure from somewhere out there on the tarmac, as she gazes through the small oval window.

"I was on the West End…"

We interrupt, "How is it out there? What's the damage like?"

"The customs office was wiped out. It's chaos. And so many people without food or water." She pauses again, although it seems she has more to say, and presses herself to continue.

"I saw a dinghy approach, I think from St. Thomas. They were carrying cases and cases of bottled drinking water. Someone had radioed them and told them people needed it. So they came. But custom agents wouldn't let them dock. They finally said, 'Fine, we don't need to dock. Just let us unload this water and we'll leave.' The customs agents warned them not to come near the dock, but they didn't listen. They drove by slowly and threw the cases onto the dock. And then the custom agents," she turns to face the window again, choking back fury, "they fucking threw the cases into the ocean. Every one of them. Just threw them into the water."

"Oh my God," I utter. I want to hug her but am suddenly aware of how public and out of place our grief is, in the close confines of apathetic strangers who just want to get off this plane and on their way. Instead I say goodbye and we disembark.

At the Newark airport, a sunburnt portly American couple seated across from us complain about being stranded for days at a hotel near a cruise ship port somewhere in the Caribbean. Their flights were canceled repeatedly due to the hurricanes, their holiday cruise and vacation from life stretched far beyond their comfort zone, and the middle aged Southern man worries about missing so much work. Adam and I sit mute, resigned to our own exhaustion and nodding to sleep in our chairs. The woman next to us speaks up vehemently, in a quick agitated island accent.

"Well, I'm from St. Thomas. And I was there when Irma hit. And it was no joke. Water just came flooding in, destroyed my grandmother's house. We had to run to the second floor where the roof started flying off. St. Thomas is destroyed. Just destroyed."

These complaints resonate with us enough to earn our attention and our commiseration.

"You were in St. Thomas? We were in Tortola." We begin sharing stories, sympathy, misery and shock. The St. Thomian woman is visibly still shaken. The couple joins the conversation, humbled and apologetic.

"Wow, we have nothing to complain about. We are very sorry for you guys. Glad you made it out alive."

When my brother David picks us up from the airport that evening, we see his own embodiment of Irma and begin to gain some idea of the toll the last week has taken on our families. Despite his sunken eyes and weary smile, he hugs us with such fervor, it feels as though we are not just returning from the Caribbean, we are back from the dead. On the drive to his house, he speeds around an exit ramp, and my heart palpitates as I grip the seat.

"Please slow down, David. I don't want to die on the way home." It must have sounded overdramatic at the time, but over-drama was exactly what our psyches had grown accustomed to. Like an abused child who flinches at a raised hand, I was now programmed to brace for trauma, and it would take me quite some time before I would be deprogrammed.

Cruising at a safer speed through residential Raleigh neighborhoods, I stare at every structure, scrutinizing and postulating, *That roof would never survive Irma. Those windows would be smashed to pieces. That flimsy house would be blown apart.* Adam who sits quietly in the backseat tells me later that he had been thinking the same.

Back at David's beautiful three-story condo, a recent purchase and symbol of my baby brother's responsible choices in life (unlike our own), we drink cold beers and Adam and I chain-smoke on the patio. I cannot sleep, nor will I be able to for days. In fact, it will be months until either Adam and I enjoy a full night's sleep, unencumbered by nightmares or anxiety.

Laying on David's black leather couch with a ceiling fan and air-conditioning panting to cool my feverish mind, inflamed with embers of guilt, helplessness and urgency to check on friends, to communicate, to see what people need and figure out how to get it to them; I am startled to hear the doorbell ring. It is my mother who has flown on a last-minute flight from Erie to Raleigh. She could not wait even a day to hug her daughter and her son-in-law. We both cry and talk well into the morning. My mom tells me repeatedly how worried she was, how obsessively my entire family worked to get us out of there. I tell her about Irma, and as difficult as it is for my poor mom to hear, that I thought I was going to die.

CHAPTER 12: IRMA IS STILL HERE

For months Adam and I drift from house to house, family to family, friend to friend. We sleep lightly, roused by a blowing air-conditioning vent into terror. We imagine every neighborhood 99 percent leveled, newly gifted by Irma with the unique ability to transpose cataclysmic destruction on any setting—a shopping centre, a friend's kitchen, a park, an entire town.

Nearly two months after fleeing Tortola, a freak tornado tears through Erie, Pennsylvania, during a Thanksgiving feast. I beg my family to hide in the basement. They refill their wine glasses and mute that pesky PSA red alert tornado warning blaring from the television. (Sadly, the tornado did end up killing two Erie residents who drowned from flooding while hiding in their basement.)

For the ensuing months of our displacement, Adam and I watch our dismal days unfold without the expansive Caribbean sea, without the omnipresent sun, without the lush rolling hills thick with palm trees, and without tree frogs telling us to dream. We miss our "Good mornings" to strangers, communal commutes, impromptu Soca dance parties and our Sunday sunsets. We miss our friends, our jobs, our daily routines, our own bed. I miss calling "5-6-7-8" to the countless students who chasséd, shimmied and wined their waists across the studio floor of the BVI Dance

School, which was halved by Irma's blow. I try to write a book, an homage to this special time, a testament to what was lost. I cry and cry and cry.

Hurricane Irma pressed a reset button for the British Virgin Islands and the people who call (or called) it home. What we are being "reset" to, remains to be determined. Although this feels like a long, dark chapter, it is only the beginning. I am clearly luckier than others in having the space, the time, the support of family to write this book, as friends back in Tortola raced to get roofs back on their homes before another hurricane strike. As Adam and I take our first steps towards rebuilding our lives, still feeble and depressed and shell-shocked by the sudden dismantling of our reality; the islands struck by Irma, Jose and Maria continue to crawl on scabby knees towards their new reality. Their difficulties go beyond rebuilding, which in itself will take several years, particularly if expected to meet the unrealistic standards necessary to withstand increasingly volatile hurricanes like Irma.

The new reality of these islands, and many parts of the world now more threatened than ever by catastrophic natural disasters caused by climate change, may be one of a long, futile struggle against forces beyond their control: a gradual depopulation as fewer and fewer residents brave out more destructive hurricanes, and fewer still choose to stick around to rebuild; an irreversible devegetation as uprooted flora go unplanted, or do not have the chance to thrive before being ravished again by another hurricane; extinction or migration of local fauna as they lose their habitats; and economic collapse as businesses deem investment in such a fragile financial environment too risky. Meanwhile the developed world grossly over-consumes the Earth's natural resources and spews waste and CO_2 emissions into our environment at a rate scientifically-proven to be disastrous for us all, defecating on our precious planet and leaving the innocent to bear the consequences.

To anyone fortunate enough to have visited or resided in a place as beautiful and special as the British Virgin

Islands, this new reality is unacceptable. To allow such a place, a people, a way of life and culture to slide permanently into the world's memory bank is unconscionable. What will it take before we take heed? Must we wait until we are hiding in our bathtubs, pummeled by ungodly winds sucking the roofs and skulls from our beings before we are willing to open our eyes?

May Irma go down in history as the worst hurricane ever to strike land in the Caribbean. May we be jammin' still, years from now, with the memory of her as an unparalleled catastrophe. May we treasure what is beautiful and what is dear to us, and may we do whatever is in our power to preserve and protect it.

I foolishly believed that with the conclusion of this book, I would finally be able to put Irma behind me. The truth is, she will be with me always, her dust in my bones, her winds in my ear, her message to us all, like a giant piece of flying debris, lodged permanently in my heart. She has inscribed my soul indelibly. Irma is here to stay.

THE END

OTHER WORLDWIDE RECORD-BREAKING NATURAL DISASTERS, ANOMALIES AND EVENTS OF 2017-2019

2017

FEBRUARY: Northeastern Brazil experiences worst drought in history.[8]

APRIL-MAY: Northern California experiences wettest winter in a century.[9]

Oklahoma, Arkansas and Missouri report record-high water levels from flooding.[10]

JULY: British Columbia experiences its worst wild fires in recorded history.[11]

---

[8] Brueck, Hilary. "Natural disasters set records around the world in 2017 — these were the worst." Business Insider. 24 December 2017. https://www.businessinsider.com/worst-natural-disasters-hurricane-flood-wildfire-2017-12#the-dry-conditions-that-fueled-flames-in-some-spots-also-perpetuated-long-term-drought-in-others-8

[9] "Northern California Just Surpassed the Wettest Year on Record." Scripps Institution of Oceanography. University of California San Diego. 13 April 2017. https://scripps.ucsd.edu/news/northern-california-just-surpassed-wettest-year-record

[10] Irfan, Umair and Brian Resnick. "Megadisasters devastated America in 2017. And they're only going to get worse." Vox. 26 March 2018. https://www.vox.com/energy-and-environment/2017/12/28/16795490/natural-disasters-2017-hurricanes-wildfires-heat-climate-change-cost-deaths

[11] Brown, Scott. "Province says 2017 is B.C.'s worst wildfire season on record." Vancouver Sun. 16 August 2017. https://vancouversun.com/news/local-news/province-says-2017-is-b-c-s-worst-wildfire-season-on-record

AUGUST: Hurricane Harvey breaks the record for a single tropical cyclone rainfall in U.S. history.[12]

SEPTEMBER: Puerto Rico begins what will be the longest blackout in U.S. history due to the impact of Hurricane Maria.[13]

San Francisco sets record for highest-temperature streaks and warmest weather ever.[14]

OCTOBER: Tubbs fire becomes most destructive fire in California history.[15]

DECEMBER: Thomas fire becomes the largest fire on record in the state of California.

---

[12] Blake, Eric S. and David A. Zelinsky. "Hurricane Harvey." National Hurricane Center Tropical Cyclone Report. National Weather Service. National Oceanic and Atmospheric Administration. 9 May 2018. https://www.nhc.noaa.gov/data/tcr/AL092017_Harvey.pdf

[13] Irfan, Umair. "It's been more than 100 days and Puerto Rico is still in the longest blackout in US history." Vox. 4 January 2018. https://www.vox.com/energy-and-environment/2017/10/30/16560212/puerto-rico-longest-blackout-in-us-history-hurricane-maria-grid-electricity

[14] Samenow, Jason. "San Francisco smashes all-time record high temperature, hits 106 degrees." 1 September 2017. https://www.washingtonpost.com/news/capital-weather-gang/wp/2017/09/01/san-francisco-smashes-all-time-record-high-temperature-hits-106-degrees/?utm_term=.1966800379c1

[15] "Stats and Events." Cal Fire. California Government Department of Fire and Forestry Protection. http://www.fire.ca.gov/communications/downloads/fact_sheets/Top20_Acres.pdf

In 2017, Earth experiences its warmest year on record without an El Niño event, according to National Oceanic Atmospheric Administration.[16]

185 major weather stations beat their all-time highest temperature records, and 17 beat records for their all-time lowest temperature.

Fourteen nations set or tied all-time national heat records:

Mezaira, United Arab Emirates

Caloane Island, Macau

Wetland Park, Hong Kong

Serravialle, San Marino

Ahwaz, Iran

Hayaya, Comoros

Roma Macao AWS, Vatican City

Quiryat, Oman

Turbat, Pakistan

Koundara, Guinea

Navrongo, Ghana

Cauquenes, Chile

Cocos Islands, Australia

All-time national cold records set in 2017:

Jabel Jais, United Arab Emirates

Abu Samra, Qatar

2018

JULY-AUGUST: Japan hits a record high temperature of 106 degrees Fahrenheit, according to the Japan Meteorological Agency.[17]

---

[16] Masters, Dr. Jeff. "NOAA: Earth Had Its Third Warmest Year on Record in 2017." 18 January 2018. https://www.wunderground.com/cat6/noaa-earth-had-its-third-warmest-year-record-2017

[17] Meixler, Eli. "Deadly Japan Heat Wave Continues as Temperatures Reach Highest Ever." Time. 23 July 2018. http://time.com/5345553/japan-heat-wave-record-temperatures/

AUGUST: Mendocino fire becomes the largest fire on record in the state of California, beating the record set eight months prior.[18]

The following cities break all-time heat records:[19]

Denver, Colorado	Belfast, Northern Ireland
Tbilisi, Georgia	Burlington, Vermont
Yerevan, Armenia	Montreal, Quebec
Glasgow, Scotland	Quiryat, Oman
Shannon, Ireland	Several cities in Russia
Mt. Washington, New Hampshire	

Germany experiences the driest summer and fall on record. In Hungary, the water levels of the Danube River hit record lows.[20]

OCTOBER: Baltimore has record high rainfall.

NOVEMBER: Camp Fire becomes deadliest, most destructive fire in California's history.[21]

---

[18] Hauser, Christine and Sarah Mervosh. "Mendocino Fire Reaches Record Size in California." New York Times. 7 August 2018. https://www.nytimes.com/2018/08/07/us/mendocino-complex-fire-california.html

[19] Samenow, Jason. "All-time heat records have been set all over the world this week." Independent. 5 July 2018. https://www.independent.co.uk/environment/heatwave-temperature-records-broken-europe-north-america-eurasia-middle-east-latest-a8432226.html

[20] Kotecki, Peter. "Natural disasters set records around the world in 2018. These were some of the worst." 6 December 2018. https://www.businessinsider.com/worst-natural-disasters-records-world-in-2018-2018-11

[21] "Northern California Just Surpassed the Wettest Year on Record." Scripps Institution of Oceanography. University of California San Diego. 13 April 2017. https://scripps.ucsd.edu/news/northern-california-just-surpassed-wettest-year-record

2018 marks the most-active hurricane season on record.[22]

2019

JANUARY: Thirty-three temperature stations in the southern hemisphere experience all-time record high temperatures (September 2018-January 2019).[23]

Caribou, Maine beats its record for yearly snowfall.[24]

FEBRUARY: The Mississippi River and Tennessee Valley experience record rainfall. Flagstaff, Arizona has snowiest single day on record. Hawaii experiences record winds, waves and snow due to intense winter storm. Record snowfall and cold temperatures spread from states Washington to Wisconsin.[25]

MARCH: Western Iran has unprecedented rainfall. Australia experiences its hottest March on record.[26]

---

[22] Gibbens, Sarah. "2018's Deadly Hurricane Season, Visualized." National Geographic. 20 December 2018. https://www.nationalgeographic.com/environment/2018/12/hurricane-season-explained-maps-photos/

[23] Nace, Trevor. "So Far 2019 Has Set 33 Hottest And 0 Coldest Temperature Records." Forbes. 31 January 2019. https://www.forbes.com/sites/trevornace/2019/01/31/so-far-2019-has-set-33-hottest-and-0-coldest-temperature-records/#2886ad49505e

[24] "National Climate Report - January 2019." NOAA National Centers for Environmental Information, State of the Climate: National Climate Report for January 2019, published online February 2019, retrieved on July 28, 2019 from https://www.ncdc.noaa.gov/sotc/national/201901

[25] "National Climate Report - February 2019." NOAA. Report for February 2019, published online March 2019, retrieved on July 28, 2019 from https://www.ncdc.noaa.gov/sotc/national/201902

[26] "Global Climate Report - March 2019." NOAA. March 2019, retrieved on July 27, 2019 from https://www.ncdc.noaa.gov/sotc/global/201903

United States has wettest winter on record.[27]

Rockford and Moline, Illinois experience coldest temperatures on record.[28]

Record floods occur along Missouri, Mississippi, and Platte rivers due to ice jams, heavy rainfall, and rapid snowmelt.[29]

Alaska experiences warmest March on record.

APRIL: In Alaska, Kotzebue has warmest April on record, and Tanana and Kutsokwim rivers have earliest ice breakup on record.[30]

Arctic sea extent is smallest for April in history of satellite records.

MAY: Average Antarctic sea-ice coverage is the smallest on record for May.[31]

---

[27] "U.S. records wettest winter capped by a cooler, wetter February 2019." National Oceanic and Atmospheric Administration. US Department of Commerce. 6 March 2019. https://www.noaa.gov/news/us-records-wettest-winter-capped-by-cooler-wetter-february-2019

[28] Wong, Sam. "So far 2019 has set 35 records for heat and 2 for cold." 30 January 2019. https://www.newscientist.com/article/2192369-so-far-2019-has-set-35-records-for-heat-and-2-for-cold/

[29] "National Climate Report - March 2019." NOAA. Retrieved on July 28, 2019 from https://www.ncdc.noaa.gov/sotc/national/201903

[30] "National Climate Report - April 2019." NOAA. Report for April 2019, published online May 2019, retrieved on July 8, 2019 from https://www.ncdc.noaa.gov/sotc/national/201904

[31] "May 2019 was the 4th hottest on record for the globe. Antarctic sea ice coverage shrank to a record low last month." NOAA. 18 June 2019. https://www.noaa.gov/news/may-2019-was-4th-hottest-on-record-for-globe

Israel experiences record-breaking high temperatures and Japan sets a new May maximum temperature record.

JUNE: The European-average temperature for June 2019 is higher than for any other June on record.[32]

South America and Bahrain experience their hottest June on record. Hawaii experiences its highest June temperature departure from average on record.[33]

JULY: On July 4th, several locations throughout southern Alaska beat all-time records for high temperatures, including Anchorage, which reached 90 degrees Fahrenheit.[34]

The Arctic experiences wildfires that are unprecedented in size and intensity.[35]

Both NOAA and NASA declare July of 2019 as Earth's hottest month on record.[36]

---

[32] "Record-breaking temperatures for June." The Copernicus Climate Change Service (C3S). 2 July 2019. https://climate.copernicus.eu/record-breaking-temperatures-june

[33] "Global Climate Report - June 2019." NOAA National Centers for Environmental Information, State of the Climate: Global Climate Report for June 2019, published online July 2019, retrieved on July 27, 2019 from https://www.ncdc.noaa.gov/sotc/global/201906

[34] "ALL-TIME High Temperature Records Set! July 4, 2019." National Weather Service Anchorage. 5 July 2019. 8:53 a.m. http://twitter.com/NWSAnchorage

[35] "CAMS monitors unprecedented wildfires in the Arctic." Copernicus Atmosphere Monitoring Service (CAMS). 11th July 2019. https://atmosphere.copernicus.eu/cams-monitors-unprecedented-wildfires-arctic

[36] Donegan, Brian and Bob Henson. "July 2019 Was Earth's Hottest Month on Record, NOAA Concludes." The Weather Channel. 15 August 2019. https://weather.com/news/climate/news/2019-08-15-july-earths-hottest-month-record-noaa-state-of-climate-report

Tortola Dance Project prepares to march on Water Front Drive in the annual Emancipation Day Festival Parade, August 7th, 2017, unaware that Tortola's most historic rainfall is about to flood the island. Photo credit: Steve McGann

On August 7th, day of Emancipation Day Festival Parade, cars throughout Road Town become submerged in floodwater. Seventeen inches of rain fall in seventeen hours.

West view from our balcony, overlooking Cane Garden Bay and
the islands of Sandy Cay and Jost Van Dyke, before Irma.
Photo credit: Diandra Jones

Cane Garden Bay residents on beach before Irma. Local dogs,
a.k.a. "coconut retrievers," Tanner and Victor.
Photo credit: Diandra Jones

View of Cane Garden Bay from Soldier Hill, before Irma.
Photo credit: Leslie Cramer

Cane Garden Bay residents wander through the ruins of the now
desolate main road, after Irma. Photo credit: Leslie Cramer

Destruction along the main road through Cane Garden Bay, a semi-trailer truck hauling a container, rolled by Irma's strength. Photo credit: Robert Shifman

Cars flung onto the hillside, stripped of vegetation by Irma's 178+ mph winds. Photo credit: Geronimo Jones

Hurricane-proof concrete home in Cane Garden Bay, built to
withstand category-5 winds, eviscerated by Irma.
Photo credit: Leslie Cramer

Concrete, steel structures gutted by Irma in Road Town.
Scotiabank in the background. Photo credit: Geronimo Jones

Cars flipped by Irma's winds and stacked on one another in carpark of Village Cay Marina, Road Town.
Photo credit: Diandra Jones

Residents climb through debris in Road Town, trying to salvage belongings and garner resources to fortify their homes for ensuing hurricanes. Photo credit: Geronimo Jones

British helicopters arrive to assist with rescue, security and recovery efforts. Photo credit: Geronimo Jones

A sixty-two foot catamaran, weighing 33 tons (or 66,000 lbs), is launched by Irma and lands on top of the guard station at Nanny Cay Marina. Photo credit: Leslie Cramer

British soldiers patrolling area near Queen Elizabeth Park.
Photo credit: Geronimo Jones

Dancer Sara Smith in what remains of the BVI Dance School
studio in Manuel Reef. Photo credit: Kemuel Gumbs

Cane Garden Bay residents spread positive vibes with graffiti on wall outside what was the local watering hole, Paradise Club. Rhymers hotel in the background. Photo credit: Ron Cline

Diandra tearfully hugs their pilot Darrin Benton. Photo credit: Adam Stauffer

At Luis Munoz Marin International Airport, hundreds of Puerto Rican volunteers welcome trauma-stricken Irma survivors from neighboring islands (estimated 5000 per day), hold signs, hand out toiletries, clothing, toys, and lend their personal cell phones. Eight days after this picture is taken, on September 20, 2017, Puerto Rico is devastated by Hurricane Maria. This book is dedicated to the people of Puerto Rico who opened their arms to disaster refugees, only to be left bereft in their own time of need. Photo credit: Diandra Jones

Satellite IR image shows Hurricane Irma near peak intensity, afternoon of September 6th, above the BVI. Maximum sustained winds 185 MPH, central pressure 914 mb on the 5 pm EDT NHC advisory. Courtesy of CIMSS, University of Wisconsin-Madison.

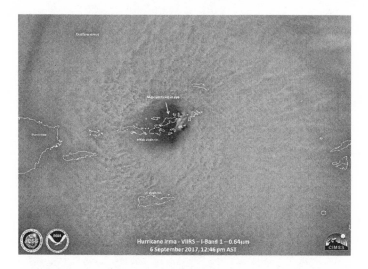

BVI in the eye of Irma. Image taken by VIIRS on board the Suomi National Polar-orbiting Partnership and NOAA-20 weather satellites, 12:46 pm, on September 6th, 2017, with annotation. Courtesy of Will Straka, CIMSS, University of Wisconsin-Madison

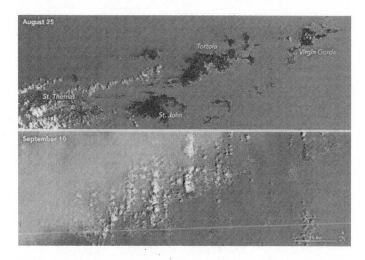

NASA's landsat-8 satellite images, before & after Irma, show the rapid deforestation of the US and British Virgin Islands by Irma's destructive winds. Source: https://www.weather.gov/tae/Irma_technical_summary

Diandra and Adam on wedding day, June 3rd, 2017, three months before Irma. Photo credit: Jeremy DeBauche

Diandra and Adam in a tighter embrace, having arrived safely at Luis Munoz Marin International Airport in Puerto Rico on September 12, 2017, on the first US evacuation G5 jet from the BVI, pictured behind them.

ABOUT THE AUTHOR

Diandra Jones is a writer, interdisciplinary artist, dancer and choreographer who has spent most of her adult life traveling, teaching and studying places geographically and culturally foreign to her hometown of Erie, Pennsylvania. After retiring from a career as a professional Irish Step dancer, Diandra taught English and Dance in Chicago Public Schools before residing for ten years in Ghana, West Africa, then the U.S. and British Virgin Islands. She currently lives with her husband in Honolulu, Hawaii. Much of her life work, whether in teaching, performance or in writing, has sought to bridge gaps in intercultural understanding to engender in her fellow humans compassion for one another and for their environment. She is a Cum Laude Honors graduate of Loyola University with a B.A. in English Literature, and holds an M.A. in Interdisciplinary Arts from Columbia College Chicago.